a feng shui guide for young adults

Fun Shway

CHANGE YOUR ROOM, CHANGE YOUR LIFE!

INESSA FREYA

Editors: Colette DeDonato, Amie Norris, John Seeley, Valerie Porter
Illustrator: Emma Fourie
Cover and book design by Asya Blue Design.

ISBN 979-8-9886868-0-4 Paperback
ISBN 979-8-9886868-1-1 Ebook

A NOTE TO THE READER

Fun Shway is my gift to you. It's the book I wish I had when I was a young adult. Fun Shway is a system of mindfully arranging your space with intention. It's about elevating you and your space into the highest vibration and co-creating your destiny. It's my wish that you find at least one thing in this book that you can use to create an amazing and meaningful life!

Love,
Inessa

CONTENTS

My Room Is a Mess and So Am I!

My Room Is a Mess, and So Am I!

Every young adult has a unique relationship with his or her room. I certainly had mine. Apparently, my goal was to win the world record for the messiest room on the planet. I couldn't walk through my bedroom without stumbling over my jeans or an empty bag of Doritos. It was a perfect illustration of everything that was happening inside of me—the good and the bad. I used the TV noise to muffle my negative thoughts and made messes—piles of belongings stretched from one end of my room to the other—to distract myself from my uncomfortable feelings.

High school was a difficult place and time for me. I was depressed most of the time but didn't know it. I attended three different schools, each time thinking the next would be better. I never felt like I fit in any of them. The problem was me. At fifteen, I asked my parents to send me to a Catholic girls' school because

I felt like I needed more discipline and structure—mind you, I am Jewish! After just one year, I was already in trouble for not wearing my green knee-highs on Mass Wednesdays and for turning my classmates on to self-help concepts. Imagine that!

While most of the girls in the locker rooms were bracing their bodies with bras, I was bracing mine with control top underwear. My body was not what I had imagined it would become after puberty (surprise!). So, how did I deal with my body image?

One, I avoided looking at it. Two, I left all my clothes on the floor, acting out against the body they were supposed to cover. I never hung my clothes up in a way that I could enjoy or appreciate, and it took me forever to get ready in the morning because I couldn't find anything. My room was a black hole that things mysteriously disappeared into.

The growing stacks of paper and unfinished projects on my desk became unfortunate reminders of all the things I couldn't get done, as well as everything that I had been holding onto for years. I kept telling myself that one day I would get around to finishing what I'd started, but that day never came.

My mother, a neat freak, would come into my room when I wasn't home and attempt to bring order to the chaos. Sometimes she would throw things away and I would rebel by creating a bigger mess—again and again. As a young adult, your room is the closest you get to having your own personal space, and I wanted to be the only one in control of mine. But my life was out of control and so was my room. I was overwhelmed with the negative thoughts in my head, the stress in my life, and my unhealthy body image. My room reflected all these feelings, but it took me many years to see the connection.

At the time, I did not have a therapist, mentors, siblings, or emotionally mature friends to guide me, and my parents were immigrants who were busy making a living so that we could survive in a new country. There was no one to help me chart the rough waters of being a young adult.

When, over a decade later, I discovered the art of feng shui, my life and my room became more manageable. Moreover, making changes to my room taught me that I can consciously make changes to my life.

Does any of this sound familiar? When you look around your room, what do you see? What story does your room tell about you? What if I told you that moving just one object in your room with intention could help you feel better about yourself? What if I told you that you could clear one single drawer and its clutter, and this could give you the energy to finish a project you've been putting off?

Maybe your room is semiorganized, and you know where most things are, but there are things in your life that you want to change or improve. Maybe there is another version of who you are that's dying to come out, and it just needs an invitation.

Had anyone ever told me that I could make simple changes to my bedroom, and that somehow those small things could change my life—my feelings, thoughts, and overall attitude—I would have started this journey much earlier than I did. So here is your chance!

What if I told you magic is real? It seems so when you begin to see the world as a system of energy in constant vibration. Your room has immense power, and by mindfully rearranging it, you can achieve your goals faster and easier and feel more at peace in your life.

The process I'm going to share with you goes way beyond your physical space. Your room is just a starting point. I will teach you skills, so that you can use the power of your mind to bring greater well-being and harmony into your life. If you want to succeed in anything in life, you must start with the first step. In this case, you don't have to go any farther than your own bedroom. This book is a great place to start your own journey.

Enjoy!

CHAPTER 1

Show Me the Shway!

"So, what is feng shui?"

I'm glad you asked. First, it's pronounced "fuhng sh-way" and is an ancient art that originated in China three to four thousand years ago. It's about how we humans interact with our environment and how we can create spaces that fill our lives with harmony and balance. There are as many schools of feng shui as there are lattes at Starbucks, and each has its own distinct flavor and essence. In this book, I'm going to venture way beyond traditional feng shui to show you **Fun Shway**—my own blend of this ancient Chinese art plus lessons from psychology, spirituality, intuition, and fun. The tools and techniques I've compiled into this book have been shared with clients of all ages and life stages over the last fifteen years.

Show
ME THE
Shway!

Feng shui works like a balancing act between you, your environment, and the world around you.

"So, if that's feng shui, what exactly is Fun Shway?"

Fun Shway is what I call it. It's my take on this ancient art. Fun Shway will teach you how to make the most of your bedroom, so that you can get the most out of life. Once you take charge of your room and make powerful changes, you will be surprised at how much you can shape your life and your future.

You become the co-creator of your destiny!

"I'll become the co-creator of what?"

Have you ever felt like your life is just happening to you and you don't have much control over how it unfolds? Do you sometimes feel like a victim? Like the whole world is against you?

Becoming a co-creator of your destiny means that all that can stop. It means you can shape your life and bring about the circumstances that you are meant to have. Once you see that you are the co-creator of your life, then the ripples of events and the synchronicities that you never saw as being possible will begin to occur.

"Okay, but who am I co-creating my life with?"

Whatever you want to call it (e.g., God, the Universe, Source, Universal Energy, Holy Spirit, Jesus, Buddha, Allah, etc.), there is a force much larger than you. This force is always trying to work *with* you and *through* you for your highest good. Working with this higher power, in other words "co-creating," means you will be guided through life; it will feel like you are flowing. You won't have to push so hard. You have much more to learn about your space and its impact on you. Maybe you would like to be more creative, organized, aware, and in charge of things, but you have never been quite sure how to do it. Making changes can seem overwhelming or scary. But never fear, Fun Shway is here.

Oh, and another thing. In this book we're going to talk about **Inner Shway** and **Outer Shway**. In Fun Shway, we work on two levels: the inner (your mind) and the outer (your room). To get the most out of this work, **it's important to make changes on the inside while you make changes to the outside**. This means you work on your inner life and your physical space at the same time. We're going to call this your...

Inner Shway & Outer Shway

Inner Shway

Inner Shway is the mental, emotional, and spiritual (internal) work you do to live your best life. It's your attitudes, beliefs, thoughts, and patterns. The better you get at Inner Shway, the easier it will be to achieve what you want in life.

Outer Shway

Outer Shway is the physical (external) expression of everything you experience on the inside. It's your bedroom, relationships, and the positive action you create in the world that will help you realize your dreams.

When I began Fun Shway, I only focused on my bedroom, but by making changes in the bedroom I recognized that changes were also occurring in my life.

I made a change in one area of my room and very soon noticed that changes started happening in my life. There was a connection! Outer reality reflected inner reality. Cleaning out an old filing cabinet or a dresser crammed full of stuff gave me a much-needed spark of energy. Where I felt bogged down and depressed before, I now had openness, clarity, and enthusiasm! But that's just one example. There have been so many synchronicities over the years that I've stopped counting.

It's cause and effect, or a feedback loop: what happens in your room will impact what happens in your life experience. Since everything is interconnected, you can rewrite the script of your life and break patterns by making changes to your room. The results aren't always apparent right away, but once it's happened enough times, it will become undeniable!

It's an amazing system designed by the universe to show us how we are doing and to keep us always learning and growing. Learning more about Fun Shway will show you how to create an environment that inspires you and brings balance and harmony to your life.

Before you take the first few steps on this amazing adventure, I'd like to share a few powerful ideas that you'll want to take with you on any important journey you make in your life

Change Your
Attitude,
Change Your
Life!

CHAPTER 2

Change Your Attitude, Change Your Life

Fun Shway is as much about rearranging our thoughts and beliefs as it is about rearranging our rooms. In fact, once you start making changes to your room, you might find it changes the way you look at your life.

You may not have control over everything that happens, but you do have one hundred percent control over how you respond to what happens. In other words, it's not your issues that are the problem—it's the way you react to them. Looking more closely at the attitude you bring to your life and how you treat yourself can help you see what is holding you back from living up to your potential.

Soon you'll be taking notes about your environment, starting with your room. Before you do, I want to give you a framework meant to help you while you're reading this book. Being aware of these things will help ensure your success.

1. All Change Starts With You

When you change your relationship with yourself, your relationship with the world around you will shift also. Here are areas of your life to start examining:

> A) Repetitive patterns, like fear of speaking up and asking for what you really want
>
> B) Old habits that are not serving you, such as procrastination and not keeping your word
>
> C) Communicating authentically, like asking for what you need and establishing healthy boundaries

Recognizing these things doesn't mean you need to feel bad about yourself; it just means you are becoming more self-aware.

2. Adopt a Beginner's Mind

When we become know-it-alls we close ourselves off from true growth and learning. If you pay attention and adopt a beginner's mind, which means a mind that is curious and humble, you may learn something—really learn something—that transforms every part of your existence in a positive way.

3. Take Small Steps

The Chinese philosopher Lao-Tzu said, "A journey of a thousand miles begins with one step." Consider that you have taken the first step with the purchase of this book. Congratulate yourself for that. Success rarely happens overnight. Thomas Edison made a thousand unsuccessful attempts at inventing the light bulb before getting it right, Bill Gates didn't build Microsoft in a week, and Olympic gold medalist Michael Phelps didn't win twenty-eight medals the first time he dove into a pool. Successful people don't know exactly how they will get from A to Z, but they take baby steps and listen to the small voice inside that guides them to their heart's desire. If you continually take small steps toward your goal, you will one day reach your destination.

4. Strive for the Greater Good

Taking these small steps, becoming more self-aware, learning how to change your attitude, and creating the life you've always wanted can be fun! You may start to feel you have superpowers. Step boldly ahead, but never use your power to hurt anyone, or to control situations only for your personal gain. It's important that as you practice Fun Shway you always intend to work for the greater good. The changes you make in your own life affect everyone around you. As Gandhi said, "Be the change you wish to see in the world."

MY ROOM · MY WAY

CHAPTER 3

My Room, My Way

You might be wondering why this ancient art that originated in China three to four thousand years ago is so relevant to you now. Despite any stories you may have heard about feng shui, I won't ask you to tear down the walls of your bedroom, turn your furniture upside down, paint everything fire-engine red, or transform it into a Chinese souvenir shop. Although the results might look kind of amusing, it would also be potentially hazardous to you ever getting any rest. Plus, none of this is what feng shui—and Fun Shway—is all about!

If you're ready to learn about Fun Shway and give this practice a try, then let's get started:

1. Turn off your phone.

2. Step into your bedroom.

3. Take a few deep breaths.

4. Have a seat.

5. Spend a moment practicing being fully present.

Not sure what it means to be present? Try this: become fully aware of this moment and space. If your mind wanders to another time and place, gently escort it back to the here and now with your breath.

If you're thinking about the report you haven't finished, or getting back to the friend who messaged you, or the dinner you plan to cook, let those thoughts pass. Breathe and be still in the moment. **Put on your imaginary goggles.**

<u>Look at everything in your room as though you were seeing if for the first time.</u> Practice looking at things without judging yourself harshly.

Saying things like "I'm a mess, I'll never be able to organize anything. This is a hopeless cause, I can't believe I'm such a packrat," isn't going to help you achieve anything. For now, just look around and take notes.

Exhibit 1: Your Room

Imagine you are looking at an exhibit in a museum. What kind of objects do you see? Is there a pile of clothes that's been sitting in your room for weeks, or maybe even months? Are you still toiling away on a project that was due last week? Or perhaps there's a half-eaten gourmet meal – let's call it an 'unfinished culinary experiment' – from last week? Are there clothes you've never worn and don't plan to ever wear hanging in your closet? Or do they lie in piles all over the floor? Have those roller blades stashed under your bed for three years gone rusty? Is your desk full of clutter that makes it hard to find anything? Is the trash overflowing?

Are the walls still showcasing that band poster from high school? Or maybe there's a canvas print you chose in your early twenties that now feels out of place.

Now look at your nightstand and dresser. Are makeup, hair spray, and jewelry crowding every surface of your room?

What about in your closet? Is there so much clutter that you can't discover the floor? Fun Shway can help you organize your things and release what no longer represents you!

What's Your Style?

Your space is a canvas of your current self, ever-shifting as you navigate the chapters of your life. It's only natural for your surroundings to morph with your personal evolution. So, give yourself the freedom to let your environment echo the person you're becoming, not just the one you've been. Your room isn't just a room; it's a 3D vision board that you live in.

I bet I could tell a lot about you by just looking in your room for a few seconds, including whether your room still represents who you are today.

What's key is crafting a space that resonates with you now and nudges you toward the future you're dreaming of. Let it be fluid, let it be alive, let it be unapologetically you. Even if that means you change it a dozen times

Find
Your
Shway

TAKE the QUIZ

CHAPTER 4

Find Your Own Shway: Take the Quiz

Take the quiz and find out if your Shway is fun or in a serious funk. Circle the answers that fit best.

1. When I walk into my room, I feel...

A. Uplifted and inspired. It's a great place to bring my friends over to chill.

B. I can't wait to get out.

C. Ommmm... like it's my sanctuary.

D. Overwhelmed and confused.

E. Like I just want to fall on my bed, and sleep for a thousand years.

2. When it comes to figuring out what I'm going to wear in the morning...

A. It's easy. I've picked out my outfit the night before.

B. I just pick up whatever is on top of the mountain of clothes in my closet and that's what I wear.

C. I hate it. I can never find what I'm looking for.

D. I love it! My clothes are organized.

E. I get so overwhelmed by all the choices.

3. My bed...

A. Hasn't had a change of sheets since—um, I can't even remember when.

B. Is where I wake refreshed from a good night of sleep.

C. Is where I do homework, eat, and watch TV.

D. Is neglected since I'm never home.

E. Is very uncomfortable to sleep in.

4. Spending time alone in my room...

A. Is like a death sentence.

B. Helps me clear my mind and figure out what I really want.

C. Happens only when I'm tired of too much socializing.

D. Can be creative and fun.

E. Is boring.

5. Success to me means...

A. I have plenty of awards, trophies, and attention.

B. I feel like I am a successful person regardless of my achievements.

C. I can only feel good about myself when I meet my expectations.

D. I can only feel good about myself when I meet my parents' expectations.

E. Nothing. I don't strive for success.

6. I sleep...

A. With my iPad and/or laptop on.

B. With my teddy bear.

C. Alone.

D. With a pet.

E. What's sleep?

7. When your room is really messy, what do you do?

A. Clean it, of course!

B. Shove everything to one corner, under the bed, or into the closet.

C. Ask a parent, friend or a partner to clean your room for you

D. Nothing.

E. Wait until it becomes unbearable and then clean it.

8. If I'm upset at someone, I will usually...

A. Bury the feelings inside until they get so big I explode.

B. Confront the person in a calm manner.

C. Confront the person, ready to argue.

D. Tell all my friends and let them deal with it for me.

E. Feel it, release it, and move on.

9. I can see the door from my bed...

A. Completely— it's directly in front of my bed.

B. Partially—I have to crane my head.

C. Not at all.

D. Easily, because it's to the right or left of the foot of my bed.

E. I don't have a bedroom door; or, I sleep on the couch in the living room.

10. My walls reflect...

A. My favorite artists, musicians, actors, and colors.

B. My friends and family.

C. Pictures of exes, old friends, and images that no longer represent me.

D. Wallpaper from before I moved in. I can't stand it.

E. Nothing. They are bare.

11. When it comes to making a choice...

A. I ask my friends for their opinions first.

B. I check inside myself and then ask my friends for their feedback.

C. I consult with a psychic.

D. I decide on my own.

E. It's hard for me to make a decision, so I wait for my parents to make it for me.

12. My friends...

A. Are supportive, like-minded, and fun.

B. Are super sarcastic and like to pick on me.

C. Usually point out my flaws and criticize me.

D. Have very little in common with me even though we get along.

E. Are just okay.

13. My desk...

A. Is covered with food crumbs, old tissues, and stuff I don't know what to do with.

B. Is overflowing with papers and projects I need to finish.

C. Is neat and organized.

D. Is sometimes organized and other times chaotic.

E. I don't have a desk, I do my work from my bed.

14. When I sit at my desk...

A. I face a wall and my back is to the door.

B. I stare out a window and my back is to the door.

C. I'm in the same line as the door. It's directly in front of me.

D. I see the door. It's to the right or left of my desk.

E. The door is on the same wall as the desk and I can see it if I turn my head.

Once you're finished, please assign these numbers to your answers and add up your score.

1.	2.	3.	4.	5.
A. 5	A. 5	A. 3	A. 1	A. 3
B. 1	B. 2	B. 5	B. 5	B. 5
C. 4	C. 1	C. 4	C. 3	C. 4
D. 2	D. 4	D. 2	D. 4	D. 2
E. 3	E. 3	E. 1	E. 2	E. 1

6.	7.	8.	9.	10.
A. 2	A. 5	A. 1	A. 3	A. 4
B. 3	B. 4	B. 4	B. 4	B. 5
C. 5	C. 3	C. 2	C. 2	C. 1
D. 4	D. 1	D. 3	D. 5	D. 2
E. 1	E. 2	E. 5	E. 1	E. 3

11.	12.	13.	14.
A. 3	A. 5	A. 1	A. 1
B. 5	B. 2	B. 2	B. 2
C. 1	C. 1	C. 4	C. 3
D. 4	D. 4	D. 3	D. 5
E. 2	E. 3	E. 5	E. 4

How Fun Is Your Shway?

If you scored 49–70 points: Pretty Fab Shway!

You and your room are totally in alignment with the universal flow of energy, and you pretty much manifest and create at will. Your room empowers you and you know how to keep yourself in a positive frame of mind most of the time. However, you're human, and like all humans you're prone to flailing around occasionally. Fun Shway gives you some super cool tools to help you to reach your full potential.

If you scored 31–48 points: Your Shway Could Use Some Fun!

When things are going your way, your space is amazing. When they don't, you feel like life has knocked you down and you have a hard time getting up again—and your room reflects your moods. What you're longing for is balance and serenity. Your Shway could really use some fun and harmony. Although you're pretty good at creating what you want in life, Fun Shway will support you in feeling like you're a co-creator of your destiny.

If you scored 14–30: The Funk Has Got Your Shway!

Life feels like it's happening to you most of the time, and your room is a reflection of the windstorm that hit last week, and the week before, and last month. You generally feel out of control and wish someone, or something, would help you see your life differently. The good news is that Fun Shway is a great first step into gaining mastery over your mind and life. This book is definitely for you!

Keys to Fun Shway

* Taking charge of your inner and outer space

* Releasing what no longer serves you

* Choosing the path of least resistance

* Allowing for support

* Using positive affirmations and creative visualization to attract what you want

Symptoms of Funky Shway

* Living in a cluttered room that makes you squirm just thinking about it

* Thinking you are just a bystander in your life

* Feeling overwhelmed, out of control, like a victim

* Blaming, complaining, and making excuses for your disorganized life

* Not stepping up to change attitudes and behaviors

The rest of the book is dedicated to helping you get rid of the funk and live more in the fun. It's your guide to shedding the old, embracing the new, and stepping into a life where your internal state and external surroundings mirror your joy, harmony, and the boundless possibilities that await you.

got Chi?

CHAPTER 5

Got Chi?

The Chinese believe that Chi (Qi or ch'i) is a dynamic energy that permeates all things, people, and places. It's the breath of life, the wind, water, and force behind nature. Without the concept of Chi, the art of feng shui might not have developed. Fun Shway is all about learning how to direct and gather this thing called Chi. The more Chi you have, the luckier, healthier, wealthier, and more in the flow of life you will feel. Our health and luck depend on its continued cultivation.

I like to think of Chi as a vibe. Think for a moment about the vibes you feel from people. There are some things you sense about a person that go beyond what they say and what you're seeing. This is Chi. It radiates out and precedes words. The same goes for the space you live in. You can tell a lot about people by learning to be sensitive to the Chi of their environment.

What Is This Vibe Doing in My Room?

Just like thoughts and feelings send out a vibe about you into the world, so does your room! I'm sure you've heard someone say, "Oh, she's got a great vibe," or "I got a bad vibe from that house." The speaker is usually referring to a phenomenon that's unseen but felt.

Just like people emit a personal vibe, which can be good, bad, gnarly, slick, scary, confusing, angry, or bored, so does that chair you're sitting on, the bed you sleep on, and the room you dwell in. A quick way of determining the quality of a room's Chi is to ask yourself how it makes you feel. If you like spending time in a space and if it makes you feel lighter, that is probably an indicator of Chi that elevates you. If you're feeling drained and tired, then the Chi may be toxic for you. The places you spend the most time in tend to have the greatest impact on your personal vibe. Tune in and ask yourself—does this space make my energy go up or down?

Once you've mindfully arranged your bedroom in alignment with the principles of Fun Shway, you will notice that the personal flow of life force energy, or Chi, will increase. And this can only mean good things!

Have you ever noticed how sometimes, for no apparent reason, you feel good and things seem to come to you without much effort? People seem friendlier and everything looks a little brighter. This means your Chi is working for you and will work faster to bring you what you need.

On the flip side, you may have noticed that when you feel sluggish and drained, it's hard to create or complete tasks. Things bother you more. People—sisters, brothers, friends, employers, teachers, relationships, even the stranger standing next to you in line to see a movie—can seem irksome, and you may find yourself more easily irritated. Draining versus empowering Chi is the difference between dry flowers and fresh flowers, a greasy countertop and one that is clean and polished, a pile of smelly laundry or clothes stacked mindfully in your closet.

This doesn't mean that everything must be perfect. I just want you to remember this: you and your room both have Chi, and they interact all of the time. The more powerful and animated your room's Chi is, the more vital you become. If you want things to change, then you must direct your Chi in ways that work FOR you rather than against you.

If you're one of those impatient people that doesn't want to wait until the middle of this book before you get started, then this is a perfect moment to jump right in. I've always been one of those readers that skims over the content looking for the activities. I learn best from a hands-on approach. If you do too, then use the two lists below to get a jump start on this creative process.

Fun Shway Time: This Chi Sucks! (But you can learn how to make it better)

* If there is something broken in your room, fix it or get rid of it. Broken items rob you of good Chi.

* DECLUTTER! Clutter drains you of your Chi.

* Dust, dirt, and grime will stagnate your Chi, especially in the corners of your room.

* Clear out the cobwebs. If you absolutely need to fill that empty place where the cobwebs once thrived, put a plant there. Watch it grow.

* Too many things in a small place choke your Chi. Too many posters on the wall, too much makeup on your dresser, too many products lining your tables or desk—all of this keeps your Chi in a holding pattern.

* Clean out the drains. Hair, soap, and—eww!—built up in your shower drains will clog up all your good Chi.

* Sharing your room or space with a messy, disorganized, clutter-lovin' person can certainly test the limits of your good Chi. There's no need for judgment, though—just a bit of creativity. Consider setting up a bookshelf as a stylish and functional divider, or hang a curtain that adds a splash of color. It's not just a boundary; it's a statement of coexistence and a testament to clever Fun Shway solutions for shared spaces.

* Don't let the darkness take over. Dark rooms can depress your Chi. Brighten your room with soft lighting or a full spectrum light bulb (this simulates natural sunlight).

* Stay away from fluorescent lights. Over time, they may contribute to a headache, or even worse, an achy migraine.

* Stop complaining. Complaining drains your Chi like nothing else! If there is someone you haven't spoken with for a while and you are holding a grudge, this can also affect your good Chi. If you can't discuss it and bury the hatchet, then the next best thing to do is to write the person a letter. Express your hard feelings and why you are upset with them, and then burn the letter.

* Get rid of what you don't use—maybe the Salvation Army needs it more—and only keep what you love. Just like there are things that animate Chi, there are also those things that drain it. Pay close attention to the things that suck your Chi!

This Chi Rules

* Add fresh flowers to your room. Throw away any dry flowers. They create a dead energy.

* Clear the heavy, tired Chi by lighting a candle, incense, or some sage. (Note: sage and incense have a strong smell that might bother some people who are sensitive to fragrance. Check in with your spacemates before using).

* Spruce up your room with some aromatherapy. Use lavender for winding down, or eucalyptus and orange for awakening your mind.

* Try to get eight hours of sleep each night to revitalize your Chi.

* Eat fresh leafy greens. This will alkalize Chi.

* Open the windows and let in some fresh Chi!

* Vacuum to collect the dust and dirty Chi.

* Put a bell on the door to invite good Chi and protect you from being startled by visitors.

* Hang things high up so your Chi, and you, will rise to new heights!

* Hang something shiny like a multifaceted crystal ball—or a disco ball—from the ceiling in the center of your room to increase Chi circulation! You can buy one from Amazon for less than ten dollars.

CHAPTER 6

Get the Funk Out

Everyone at one point or another has experienced The Funk. You ask, "How did it get here?" The truth about The Funk is that it's created by stagnant Chi.

Maybe you already have a few ideas about how and why it got stuck. The thing is, it's your choice how long you let it stay there. What you'll be learning from here on out is how you can ask it to go, how to send it on its way, how to say, "Goodbye, Funk! Don't take it personally. We're just growing apart, moving in different directions."

Here's what you might hear yourself or others say when their Chi is in a funk:

"Why me?"

"Why does this always happen to me?"

"I can't do anything right!"

Get the
Funk
Out

"Life is unfair!"

"I don't get it!"

"Nothing works!"

"I'm always confused."

"No matter how hard I try, I always fail."

"It's pointless to keep trying."

"I just have bad karma."

"My parents suck. I'm screwed, for-evah!"

You don't have to beat yourself up for having these thoughts; we all have our moments. You can transform these negative experiences into opportunities for growth. Old habits and feelings of unfairness, apathy and frustration are simply opportunities to redirect your intention onto what you do want, reminding you that it's okay to feel and that each emotion is a step towards a more conscious and heartfelt future.

With Fun Shway guiding you toward a more uplifting outlook and vibe, you'll start exuding confidence and optimism, attracting like-minded people to you. You'll see the world in a brighter light and feel equipped to handle anything that comes your way, trusting that you're moving in the right direction.

You may notice that the people who used to bring you down and suck the life force out of you—the energy vampires—become less appealing. The good news is that when you bring a little Fun Shway into your life, you open the Chi gates to receive positive energy and to those people who will love and support you and want your love and support too. You will be drawn to one another like magnets!

Getting out of The Funk and into fun means taking action. Just taking one single step in the direction of your dreams can create the momentum you'll need to manifest anything. You don't have to become an instant Fun Shway expert. Just about any type of movement gets the energy flowing: clear your clutter, take out the trash, add a new healthy plant to your desk, replace a broken light bulb, light a candle, turn off the TV, or take out your craft supplies and create something that reflects your state of mind.

Here's something to consider: **Your room is a feedback mechanism. It lets you know when something in your life is out of balance.** Here are a few things that might need changing:

* Clutter

* Broken stuff

* Outdated items

* Things you don't love

* Gifts that you don't like but hold onto because you feel guilty when you think about letting them go

Your room is the first place you can go to experience a shift in your energy.

I'm going to show you how to use your room to feel inspired, empowered, and awesome about yourself! Are you ready to minimize the time you spend in The Funk and navigate your way into happier and more fun ways of living and experiencing life? Fun Shway is about training your mind to think differently about your space. **Remember: Change your room, change your life!**

Fun Shway Time: Five Minutes to Inspire Your Chi and Get the Funk Out!

Meditating for five minutes a day will put your mind at ease and give you a healthy dose of Chi and vitality! If you've never meditated before, there's not much to it. Devote a few minutes each day to the practice of meditation.

* Find a comfortable place to sit where you won't be interrupted.

* Set your timer on your phone.

* Close your eyes.

* Sit quietly and simply focus on your breath.

* Breathe in for a count of four, hold for a count of four, and breathe out for a count of four; feel your body and mind relax. Ahhhhh.

Visualize for five minutes each morning the way you want to experience your day. As you wake up in the morning and before getting out of bed, take five minutes to imagine yourself going through the day feeling accomplished, at ease, and joyful. Imagine everything works out for you and that you have enough time to finish everything you start.

What are five things you're grateful for? For five minutes write five things you are grateful for before going to bed. It's a good way to remind yourself of all the things that are going right in your life. When you focus on what's going right, the universe gives you more reason to feel grateful.

CUTTER
WHAT'S IT DOING FOR YOU?

CHAPTER 7

Clutter: What's It Doing for You?

You can know more about a person from looking at their room for thirty seconds than from talking to them at a party for fifteen minutes. Our bedrooms send a subliminal message to the world about who we are. Ideally, your room reflects your talents, goals, and interests—your best self!

Sometimes our bad habits are easy to spot, especially when they show up as a mess on your bedroom floor. So, what do you do when the mess on the floor starts to become a way of life? You've gotten so used to it that you don't even notice it anymore. It's just

> ### There's a rule in feng shui:
>
> Everything you own, you are responsible for. This means you must be a good custodian of your possessions. If you can't take care of what you already have, then the universe won't give you anything new.

the way you roll. Eventually, the way you roll is going to get in the way. Eventually, clutter takes over.

You don't need to be a neat freak. You can have a FUN-ctional room that you love. Once you meet face-to-face with the clutter lurking in your space you will find the power within to send it packing.

What is Clutter and How Did it Get in My Room?

Clutter Defined

* Things you don't use or love

* Things that are untidy or disorganized

* Too much stuff in too small of a space

* Unfinished business

* Things that you never use or wear anymore that are taking up space

* Items that don't represent you

* Paper pileups

What is the Clutter in Your Life Costing You?

The Emotional Impact

Clutter creates shame and isolation.
> "There's no way I'm inviting anyone over!"

Clutter keeps you stuck in the past.
> "I still have my ex's watch in my nightstand, and every time I see it, I start to cry."

Clutter doesn't want harmony in relationships.
> "Someone is always yelling at me to clean my room."

The Physical Impact

Clutter can make you feel sluggish and tired.
> "I'm so bogged down and drained by all my stuff, it makes waking up in the morning hard."

Clutter affects your body weight and can make you feel depressed.
> "Who cares about what I eat? It doesn't make any difference because I feel badly already."

The Mental Impact

Clutter creates confusion.

"I can't find anything when I need it!"

Clutter causes the feeling of being overwhelmed.

"There is too much to do and I don't have time to do any of it!"

Clutter encourages procrastination.

"With a to-do list stretching all the way to Zimbabwe, it just makes me want to procrastinate even more."

The Spiritual Impact

Clutter makes it hard to live to your full potential.

"I know there's more to life than this, but I feel so bogged down."

Clutter equals baggage, and the more of it you have, the more of it you carry around in your mind. Clutter chokes, drags, drains, and overwhelms your Chi. It takes up lots of space and makes it hard for anything or anyone to enter your room or life!

The clutter in your room won't help you relax, think, or do your homework. Even if you aren't always aware of the impact clutter makes on you, I can pretty much guarantee that on some level—usually called the unconscious level—it's taking a toll on your life.

Clutter can be a red flag that there is something deeper that you're ignoring and don't want to deal with.

Perhaps you've grown comfortable with your clutter. It's just the way it is, right? Maybe you think it doesn't bother you.

Imagine wearing your favorite sneakers. They are pretty worn out and the soles have holes in them so that your feet occasionally get cold. You could throw them away, but you don't, because you've gotten so used to wearing them that you just tolerate the discomfort. Then one day you finally get yourself a new pair. And hey, they look and feel great! You can hardly believe that you tolerated the old sneakers for so long!

It's the same with clutter. We get used to our clutter, to the point that we don't notice the discomfort it causes anymore.

Let's play a game. Let's pretend your clutter is alive and can speak. Answer the question below:

Fun Shway Time

If my clutter had a voice it would say:

. . . .

. . . .

 CLUTTER

Personality Types

CHAPTER 8

Clutter Personality Types

Over the course of many years working with clients and their rooms, I found some common patterns in the ways people create clutter. The great psychologist Carl Jung saw universal "types" in human personality. Using Jung as my inspiration, I came up with "clutter personality types." Understanding these types can help you gain more awareness of your clutter style and hopefully give you more control over your room. Below each clutter personality type you will find a limiting belief that lives beneath the surface and a turbocharged affirmation that you can use to empower yourself to declutter your life.

What is a Limiting Belief?

A limiting belief is a set of ideas you adopted about yourself when you were a kid. Some of these beliefs might sound like "I'm not good enough," "I'm not smart enough," "Everything is hard for me," "People won't accept me if I make mistakes," or "I can't do anything right." There are as many limiting beliefs as there are people on this planet.

Where Do Limiting Beliefs Come From?

A limiting belief is a message about yourself that you received from your parents or a primary caregiver that inhibits your ability to flourish. It can also be something you said to yourself at a young age that restricts you in some way.

Some beliefs support you and fuel your growth. But others, like limiting beliefs, can keep you stuck in a rut and block you from achieving your creative potential.

The deepest beliefs were imprinted during the formative (first seven) years of life. As you grew older, you continued to adopt them from your culture, family, teachers, friends, and the media. Whoever and wherever they came from, they got stuck inside and now some part of you thinks they're true.

Chances are, you don't even know that you have a limiting belief. Many limiting beliefs live in the unconscious and are under your radar. A big sign that you have one is when you do the same thing repeatedly and hope for different results. For example, dating disrespectful people continually and thinking you can change them, only to find yourself brokenhearted. The limiting belief might sound something like "I don't deserve to be treated with respect and kindness," or "I can't do better so I should just settle," or "If I can only prove how amazing I am, maybe they would give me the love and affection I desire."

Let Yourself Off the Hook:

There is a great saying, "Yesterday is history, tomorrow is a mystery, and today is a gift, which is why we call it the present." Whatever has happened up until now is in the past. There's no reason to make yourself or anyone else wrong.

In most cases, a limiting belief is running the show—without you being aware of it.

Turbocharged Affirmations

After you read through each personality type, you will also find a **Turbocharged Affirmation**. You can use a turbocharged affirmation to restructure your beliefs and create new thought patterns. Saying the affirmation out loud (and placing it somewhere you can see it, like your mirror, nightstand, or desktop) will help you reprogram your mind to create a new positive belief about yourself. A new belief will create positive thoughts. I promise to elaborate more about turbocharged affirmations and how to create them in the next chapter.

Numbers That Change

In Fun Shway there are special numbers we use when we want to create a new habit. Try an affirmation for 40 days. Repeat it to yourself at least nine times a day and at most 108.

40

The number 40 has a long and sacred past. It is associated with many special events. Moses was on the mountain with God for 40 days and nights, and it rained for 40 days and 40 nights when God wanted to cleanse the world. Plus, it takes about that long to start a new habit.

Which of These Clutter Types Sounds Most Like You?

Rebellious Roxy

Roxy does not want to take orders from anyone. She might be trashing her room as an act of rebellion. For Roxy, clutter is a way of asserting her autonomy, as well as a protest against feeling controlled. Unfortunately, her fear of being controlled ultimately backfires because the clutter controls her! What Roxy really wants is more control over her life so she can experience responsible freedom.

Limiting Belief: "I feel out of control and others want to control me."

Roxy's Affirmation: "I allow myself to have control over my environment. Treating myself and my stuff with love and care helps me stay responsibly free."

How do you relate to **Rebellious Roxy?**

Flashy Franky

Franky's motto is, "You only live once, so I might as well look good." On its own this statement isn't such a bad thing, but for Franky it often means living in excess. Franky keeps buying new clothing, handbags, and shoes, then tires of them and buys some more. Instead of filling herself up from the inside, she finds her

self-worth temporarily in her Dolce&Gabbana handbag and Free People dress. Unfortunately, the "feel-good" of shopping, a.k.a. retail therapy, is short-lived and attempts to fill something much deeper that stuff can never replace.

Limiting Belief: "I'm not enough. I don't deserve to be loved for just being me."

Franky's Affirmation: "I am enough and approve of myself exactly as I am. I have a lot to offer as my true self."

How do you relate to **Flashy Franky?**

Someday Oneday Sam

Sam could be described as a sentimental collector; her room is filled with keepsakes dating back to her preschool days. She's lost track of all the items she's saved, yet she can't seem to part with any of them, believing that someday oneday, someone will want her memorabilia. Sam is caught in a scarcity mindset, not

fully recognizing the universe's generous nature, but she's slowly embracing the concept of abundance.

Limiting Belief: "There's never enough for me."

Sam's Affirmation: "I live in an abundant universe. There is always more than enough for me."

How do you relate to **Someday Oneday Sam?**

Cosmic Crystal

Crystal spends more time up in the clouds than down here with the rest of us earthlings. She is a sparkle-brain and complains that she has more ideas than time to execute them. It's hard for her to prioritize and she ends up doing five things at once—but not very successfully. Ultimately, chaos ensues in her room reflecting all the half-started tasks, which she calls "a creative mess."

Limiting Belief: There is never enough time.

Crystal's Affirmation: There is enough time for me to complete the things I start. I trust my creative process.

How do you relate to **Cosmic Crystal?**

Perfectionist Pam

Pam is good at lots of things and has multiple projects she is successfully juggling at once. But no matter how many accomplishments she has under her belt, she never quite feels good enough. She's fixated on her flaws and rarely relishes her successes. When she feels good about herself, her room is neat and tidy. When she feels bad about herself, her room is disorganized.

Limiting Belief: There's no room for mistakes. I need to be one hundred percent perfect, even if it hurts.

Pam's Affirmation: I release the need to be perfect. There's no such thing as a mistake, only opportunities to learn.

How do you relate to **Perfectionist Pam?**

Guilty Gaby

Gaby holds onto all the gifts she's received over the years. They fill her room and make her feel overwhelmed. She has a very difficult time letting go. Her excuse is that they were once a gift from her mom, dad, grandma, boyfriend, or a relative, and contain sentimental value. Every time she thinks about letting some-

thing go, she is confronted with feelings of guilt that she uses to rationalize why she can never ever part with her possessions.

Limiting Belief: If I disappoint others, I may be rejected and lose their love.

Gaby's Affirmation: It's safe for me to be true to my own needs and feelings and let go of those things I don't use, love, or need anymore. I love myself even in the face of rejection.

How do you relate to **Guilty Gaby?**

Sterile Sage

Did you know that there's another side to the clutter issue? It's when someone is too neat, and their room is void of energy, color, and inspiration.

Meet Sterile Sage. Her room looks like a hospital. She's all pent-up and afraid of making mistakes. Although she appears like she's got it together, she's playing it safe and not living life to her fullest. She cares too much about what other people think about her, and that keeps her stuck creatively.

Limiting Belief: It's not safe to express myself freely. People may not like who I really am.

Sage's Affirmation: It's okay for me to try new things and falter. Life is about discovering and evolving.

How do you relate to **Sterile Sage?**

Fun Shway Time: What Clutter Types Are Most Like You?

* What do you think are your limiting beliefs?

* How have these beliefs influenced the way you treat your room?

* What price do you pay for setting up your room this way?

* Who would you be without these limiting beliefs?

* What judgments do you make about yourself for having them?

* Are you willing to forgive yourself for any judgments you have made against yourself? If so, repeat these words: 'I forgive myself for judging myself as…' and then complete the sentence.

The Two Most Powerful Words You'll Ever Use:
I Am

CHAPTER 9

The Two Most Powerful Words You'll Ever Use: I AM

Whether you know this or not, the words you say to yourself and others have the power to shape your reality, identity, and destiny. These two words—"I am"—might seem tiny, but their impact on your life is epic. Whatever you chose to pair with "I am" tells the universe who you think you are and cements your identity.

If that seems far-fetched, let's let science do the explaining.

There's a part of your brain called the reticular activating system (RAS), a filter that sits at the base of your head and decides what information goes in and what stays out. The RAS's primary function is to guard your conscious mind, so you don't go into sensory overload from all the information that you're bombarded with all day long. How does it do that? It pays attention to whatever you're paying attention to. Like a concierge, the RAS will only let in what it thinks is important, which is based on your dominant thoughts and feelings and the words you say to yourself.

Every time you use the words "I am" you are sending a powerful declaration to your RAS to pull in all the data that matches with whatever you are affirming. For example, if one of your dominant thoughts is "I am lazy," then the RAS will focus the mind and collect all the evidence to prove this idea, whether it's true or not. You might start thinking about all the times you were late, slept in, or couldn't finish a project, and then got into a funk about it, felt sad and depressed, and didn't have the energy to finish what was in front of you. It's a vicious cycle.

When in a funk, stop and notice what you're saying to yourself, then consciously change your language to affirm your true desires. For example, instead of "I can't finish writing this section about the RAS. It's too hard," I could say, "I am easily finding the right words to complete this paragraph about the RAS with grace and ease."

Your Turbocharged Affirmations

The most effective way to communicate your desires to the universe is to make turbocharged affirmations. Affirmations are positive statements that remind you how powerful you and your words are. Your thoughts and words greatly affect your actions. Affirmations get the unconscious mind to agree with the conscious mind. Uniting them will help you achieve your goals.

The best time to say your affirmation is right before you fall asleep. That's when the unconscious mind is open and ready for new programming. Just like a computer, your brain can also be programmed. When saying your affirmation, it's helpful to couple it with an elevated emotion like joy, gratitude, or peace. A quick way to uplift your mood is to listen to inspiring music. If you find that you're beating yourself up over this exercise, or feeling stuck, perfectionism—another limiting belief that you must get it right—might be rearing its ugly head. You're going to have to let yourself off the hook. Limiting beliefs have been running the show up until now. It's time to let them go.

Writing Your Affirmations

When writing affirmations, make sure to engage your senses and use descriptive, specific language. In other words, *turbocharge* them! Can you tell the difference between a regular affirmation and one that is turbocharged?

Affirmation: I like who I am and the work I do.

Turbocharged Affirmation: I love that I am creative and insightful. I feel respected and appreciated for the work I do.

Can you see the difference? Remember, you can change your affirmation at any time, or make up new ones for the different areas of your life you want to improve.

One of the fastest ways to start believing and seeing your greatness is to write down what you desire. Writing things down also helps clarify and focus your intention on what you want instead of what you don't want. When the intention is clear, then many roads appear. In other words, "energy follows thought."
—Dan Millman

Here are some of my own personal affirmations that have helped me get through tough times.

I am a beautiful, confident woman. I allow myself to be me, and you to be you.

This was when I was feeling like I wasn't very beautiful and feeling very insecure. I had a hard time accepting myself and even judged others for their behavior. Today I believe this statement more than ever. But it really took some time and practice to let it sink in.

I am gently focused on what is right in front of me. I joyfully complete what I start.

I've always been proud of how my brain sparkles with new ideas. (Can you guess my clutter personality type?) But sometimes I can see that sparks are flying in every direction and nothing gets done. When I have twenty irons in the fire, it's challenging to bring anything to completion. When I started practicing my affirmations, I was able to see what I really needed to focus on.

Now it's time to write your own. Pick one or two areas of life where you're currently experiencing challenges and write an affirmation that supports the way you want to feel. Once you're done writing your affirmations, you can cut them out and post them around your room, read them out loud, say them to yourself quietly, read them to friends, or ask your friends to read them back to you. Say them each day.

Many people stop their affirmations because they think it's not working. I have been prone to this myself. When you have years of practice at feeling bad and talking yourself into a negative swamp, it may take some practice and commitment to trust the new statements you're making.

Don't get discouraged. Keep going. Trust me, it works!

CHAPTER 10

Unfriending Clutter

Has your clutter become the cranky guest that never leaves? If that's the case, then it's time to tell it to leave. No matter how pushy and overpowering your clutter seems to be, remember that you are stronger than you might think. It's your room and you are the one in charge. It's time you had an honest and not-so-pretty conversation with your clutter. Sure, you could try being friendly and easygoing about it. You could say, "Look, clutter, I really wish you'd leave." But by this time, your clutter has gotten used to hanging around and even feels welcome to take over your space. The gentle nudging isn't going to work.

It's time to get tough. It's time to open the door and say, "Look, clutter, I command you to leave now. Right now!"

My guess is that your unwanted guest will want to linger just a little longer, so you will need to take a little more action.

Unfriending Clutter

How to Send Clutter Packing

Get five large boxes. Depending on how much stuff you have, you may need more. Label each of them:

1. **GIVE AWAY**

2. **THROW AWAY**

3. **SELL** (on eBay, Craigslist, garage sale, or Amazon)

4. **TRANSITION** (for items that may belong someplace other than your room or in a different location in your room)

5. **COME BACK IN SIX MONTHS** (for items that you need to step away from and reconsider)

Depending on the scope of your mess, you may need to do this process in stages, which is totally cool. Invite friends over and have a clutter-clearing party. Whatever it takes!

With the five boxes at your side, pick up each object and ask the following questions:

1. Do I really USE it?

2. Do I LOVE it?

3. Does it belong here?

If the answer is "NO" to 1 and 2:
Throw it away, give it away, or sell it on eBay!

If the answer is "No" to 3:
Put it in the Transition box and move it.

If the answer is "I don't know," then...

Put it in the COME BACK IN SIX MONTHS box, date it, and come back in six months with a trusted friend who doesn't have a clutter problem. Ask your friend to hold you accountable to your intention to clear the clutter from your life. If you can't remember what's in the box, then that means it was clutter. Take out what you remember, and ask, "Do I love it or use it?" If you don't do either, then lose it!

If the answer is "yes" then...

It's a Lovable and you can keep it!!

The goal is to surround yourself with Lovables, things you truly love. (We'll talk more about Lovables in chapter 11.) Doing this will keep you focused on what's most important to you and it will keep distractions out of your way.

Energy Up, Energy Down Test

FINDING YOUR CENTER

While you're going through your belongings to determine if something is really clutter, it might help you to center in your body, which is the best barometer for how you really feel about something. Next you will do an energy up or down test to determine if the thing in question brings your energy up or drags it down. With each item ask yourself:

* Is this giving me energy? When I see this item, does it make me feel like clapping my hands or jumping around? Is this draining my energy? Do I feel tired,

like I want to fall asleep, whenever I see this thing or pick it up?

* Does this item make me feel lighter and happier, or sad and depressed?

* Does this represent who I am today, or who I was in the past?

Notice how you feel in your body while asking these questions. If you feel open and light, then most likely the item is a Lovable and you can keep it, but if your energy goes flat or just blah, then it's probably a drainer. Some things neither lift nor deplete your energy, which is okay. You can always revisit those items later.

What is one thing that you can start doing today to help manage your clutter? Example: I can spend at least five minutes before going to bed straightening out my room.

Remember, nothing gets done without taking that initial step. Don't beat yourself up if you can't clear all the clutter at once.

Clearing out a cluttered closet can surprisingly energize and uplift you, providing a sense of empowerment. Such a simple step opens up space and may encourage you to take on new challenges, like sending off a short story or strumming the first chords on a guitar. Instead of feeling overwhelmed and down, you might find yourself with a clear mind and a renewed sense of what's possible.

Making Room for Lovables

CHAPTER 11

Making Room for Lovables

Now is the time to pay attention to what you do want to keep in your life. We will call these your Lovables! Lovables are those items that give you energy, bring a smile to your face, or are simply essential to your existence, such as your computer, toothbrush, a favorite piece of jewelry, and the myriad of other possessions that live in your bedroom.

Here's a way to figure out if something is a Lovable. Get a pad of paper and make a list with these headings:

I love it!

I totally need it.

I use it.

I am inspired by this!

All the items on this list are your Lovables. Think about the items in your room and if they belong on the list, add them under the proper heading.

This may take a while, but if it's hard for you to let go of your attachment to your stuff, this process may shed light on those things you truly love and those that no longer serve you. Remember, if there are items in your room that are not listed in one of these categories, then they probably belong in one of the five boxes mentioned earlier.

Once you have made your list, check and see what you have more of in your room. How much of your room is a Lovable? How much is uninspiring or not functional? Now compare. Which do you have more of?

Now look at your life. How many people love and support you? How many people do you barely tolerate? How many situations do you find yourself in that no longer match who you are?

If you find that you are surrounded by people and situations that drain you, decide once and for all that you are ready to live a life full of love and meaning.

HAVING WHAT YOU WANT IS BLESSING WHAT YOU HAVE

Once you've released all your clutter, it's time to bathe in gratitude for everything that is amazing and awesome in your life! Gratitude is one of the fastest ways to increase your energy and become open to receive more good stuff.

Take some time right now to think about the things you are grateful for.

Saying what you are grateful for, even for a few minutes before dozing off, is a great way to shift your negative outlook toward gratitude. Your mind is most susceptible to suggestion in the few minutes before you fall asleep. Try it and you will soon see things to be grateful for everywhere!

Here are some examples:

> I'm so grateful that I have an amazing mom who loves and supports me.

> I'm so grateful that I have a healthy body that gets me where I need to go!

> I'm so grateful for my abundance of wonderful friends that are always ready to listen.

Fun Shway Time

List the things you are grateful for:

. . . .

. . . .

74

CHAPTER 12

Clear the Way for Awesome Shway

Now that you've cleared the clutter, you're ready for the next step in generating amazing vibes in your room. There are many things that can create stagnant energy in your room and deplete your Chi: old broken things, clutter, smelly laundry, and food wrappers from last semester, to name only a few. Then there are those things that are less obvious, like the emotional signature of your room.

The emotional signature of your room is based on the predominant thoughts and feelings that you have while spending time in your space. Your thoughts, emotions, and experiences literally get absorbed into the fabric of your sheets, mattress, and walls. You may have recovered from the fight or the major meltdown you had yesterday, but your room hasn't. Your room carries those memories and the issues you might be struggling with. That negative energy is still lingering on the subtle level, the realm of the invisible. Even though you can't see it, the impact can be felt deeply.

So, I'm going to ask you to treat your room with the same care and hygiene you treat yourself with.

You probably can't imagine going without a shower for a week, or a month, or a year, right? Just like you need to cleanse your body (and soul), your room also deserves a Space Clearing.

Space Clearing lifts toxic emotions and energies from the room and helps crystallize the energy so it feels sparkly and uplifting. There've been times when I'm called to Fun Shway a home and I can feel a murky cloud hanging over a person's living space. This is my first clue that the room needs an energy clearing.

Working with sound is one of the most effective tools from my space-clearing tool kit to re-energize a stagnant room. You may not know it, but low-level energy can collect in corners. One effective tool I use to break it up and clear the way is a bell or chime. The sounds from the bell or chime invite the energy to flow. Another technique is clapping, which breaks up stagnant energy (and sends the dust mites packing).

To begin the process of Space Clearing, you must set your intention. For example, "My intention is to fully clear this room of any negative energy. I do this for the highest good of all concerned." After you've set your intention, use these space-clearing tools to open the way for some great Shway.

Space-Clearing Tools to Air the Shway

Here is a list of some space-clearing tools that can be used to dissolve negative, stale, or yucky energy that has been stuck in your room.

Bells—Any bell that makes a sound you find pleasing will work. Tibetan Buddhist bells are great. If you're on a budget, then tingsha, which look like two cymbals tied together by a leather band, are low cost and work well!

Clapping—Clap in corners where the Chi gets trapped; loud clapping can work to get its attention and ask it to change its ways. Go to the corner, make a clear intention to chase away the negative or stuck energy, and clap your hands ten to thirty times.

Incense—There are many kinds of incense. If you have an aversion to strong fragrances, try more subtle fragrances like Nag Champa, traditionally used to ward off negative energy.

Sage—Sage is an ancient and sacred herb that has been used ceremonially for centuries to chase away negative energy and bad spirits. Some people call it smudging. You can find a smudge stick—typically sage, cedar, sweetgrass, and lavender bundled together—at most natural food stores. Light the tip of the smudge stick with a match or a lit candle, and then wave the stick as it smolders.

Sea Salt—Sea salt has also been used for centuries to clear low-level negative energy. Place a bowl filled with sea salt in an open space in each corner of the room. (It should be replaced after a month or so). If you have hardwood floors you can also mix five to six tablespoons of sea salt in a bucket of water and mop the floor with the mixture.

Orange—Orange and citrus scents such as mandarin and grapefruit can lift your spirit and uplift the vibe in a room. The orange symbolizes wealth and good luck. Also, the circular shape denotes wholeness and oneness. A more in-depth method as taught to me by my Feng Shui Master, Nate, is called the BTB Orange Peel Blessing and uses nine pieces of an orange peel mixed with water. This blessing marks a new beginning and is described in greater detail below in the Home Detox. You can also spray a little orange essential oil mixed with a carrier like avocado or jojoba oil to attract some sunny, auspicious, and uplifting energy into your life! You'll be using orange as one of your space-clearing ingredients, so stay tuned.

> **What's up with the number nine and why is it so special?**
>
> In numerology, nine is the number for transformation and completion. It's about the end of a cycle and preparing for the next chapter.

Calling in the Light—The white light can be called upon by anyone for healing and protection. It acts as a purifying agent that dispels funky vibrations and negative energies from your home, heart, and mind. Visualizing white light will raise positive vibes and protect you from negative emotions and thoughts that may have accumulated in your room.

> ***Instructions for calling in the light:*** Sit with a straight back. Close your eyes. Take a deep breath in through your nose and out your mouth. Feel centered in your body. Ask for white light to surround you and

your room. See it filling your body and entire space. Ask it to help you clear and remove all negativity with grace and ease.

White Candle—We light candles to set intentions for what we want to be purified and released. Candles represent fire and are used to transform negative energies. They illuminate dark spaces and remind us that even in those times when life feels difficult and we can't see where we are going, there is always a light deep inside that knows the way.

I recommend a deep Space Clearing at least once a year, or after a challenging event, such as a fight or breakup, or before moving into a new space. If you keep reading, you will find a deep space-clearing recipe called the Home Detox that I find most useful for dissolving some of those bigger issues.

The Home Detox: A Space-Clearing Recipe

The Home Detox is a space-clearing recipe that I use to clear my clients' homes. It is very powerful and best done during challenging times. It might be the very thing you need to get your energy moving again.

The process below contains many of the space-clearing tools I mentioned above and is intended for your bedroom only. To Space Clear your entire house, and all the shared spaces, requires permission from the people living with you.

The process can sometimes bring things to the surface that not everyone is ready to see. Focus on your room first. If the people who live with you see positive changes in you and ask for a clearing, then you have the green light and it's up to you how to proceed.

Items you will need for Space Clearing your room and bed:

* White candle

* A special cloth that is only used for Space Clearing (white is preferable)

* A bowl (ceramic or glass)

* An orange (easy to peel)

* Filtered or distilled water

* White sage

* Bell, Tibetan singing bowl, or tingshas (you can also use your hands to clap if you don't have any of these)

* Lighter or matches

Before you begin, a little preparation is needed. Start by opening the windows, closet, and all drawers in your bedroom. Next, you will want to find a flat surface to create an altar. This can be your desk or a nightstand. Whatever you use, make sure to clear everything off it first. An altar is a specific area designated by you as sacred during the time you're clearing your room. It's a bridge between the physical and spiritual dimensions. Here you will organize all your space-clearing items: white cloth first; then on top the sage, candle, bowl with orange, and bell. There's no right way to place the items on the altar.

There's only the way that feels best to you. Once everything is as you like it, you may begin.

INSTRUCTIONS

1. ROUND ONE—LOOSENING STAGNANT AND LOW-LEVEL ENERGIES

Stand at the front door to your room looking inside and imagine a column of white light filling and surrounding you and your room. Call on this light for protection. Call in the light OUT LOUD. You can come up with your own prayer or use the one I've provided below. Feel free to improvise or omit any words that don't match how you normally communicate. It's important to feel comfortable with this process.

"I call upon my angels, guides, ancestors, universal support, and divinity to assist me in this process of Space Clearing. I ask now for a clearing of all energies that no longer serve me. I ask for blessings of peace, joy, health, and abundance in my life right now. I place this request into the light for my highest good and the highest good of all concerned."

Starting at the door to your room, sage the entire perimeter. Use your matches or lighter to light one end of the sage. Blow out the flame gently. The sage will start smoking. Traditionally, abalone shells were used to hold the sage while it burned, and a feather was used to fan the smoke. But you can simply use a ceramic bowl to catch the ash as it burns. Waft

the sage in an upward motion. You might need to relight the sage wand several times during the process to keep it smoking. Make sure to reach all corners, under the bed, desk, and closet. Finish at the door and put your sage out. (Make sure to open at least one window before starting this process.)

2. ROUND TWO—THE PURIFICATION

Peel the skin of the orange in increments of nine so you end up with nine, eighteen, or twenty-seven pieces. (notice they all add up to nine: $1+8=9$ and $2+7=9$). You can either eat or throw away the flesh of the orange after the ritual is performed.

Place the orange skin in a bowl half full of water (distilled or filtered water is best).

Next you will use a mudra, or a specific hand gesture, to create a new circuit of energy. The one we will use is called the Karuna, or Expelling Mudra, used to expel negative energy. Take your right hand and bring together your ring finger, middle finger, and thumb, then dip your fingers in the bowl with the orange peel and water and flicker throughout your space as you walk the perimeter clockwise.

Make sure to point your fingers down, and away from you, while flickering. Continue dipping your fingers and flickering everything in your space (including the walls) as you move through your bedroom.

Next you will be using a mantra. Mantras are special words that carry vibrations. When said in a particular order they can activate positive life-changing energy. You will be using the "Om Mani Pad Mei Hum" (sounds like Oh Money

Pay Me Home), which means "The Jewel in the Lotus." This mantra honors all things, animate and inanimate, as divine and coming from the same source of oneness. If this mantra doesn't resonate, you can use your own, such as, "Cleanse all negative energy from my space now!"

3. ROUND THREE—BELLING

Using a powerful bell, a Tibetan singing bowl, or tingsha, you can now erase whatever imprints are still left over. If you don't have a bell or tingsha, you can easily order one on Amazon. Otherwise, you can clap your hands for this part.

Do another walk-through, starting at the door and going clockwise. Ring or clap, especially along the walls. Make sure you don't forget to ring or clap in all the corners and closets, as energy tends to get stuck in these areas.

4. ROUND FOUR—GRATITUDE

Stand at the door and face the interior of your room. Extend your arms out. Give gratitude to your home for all the blessings you have received and the lessons you have learned here. Ask that any further lessons be brought with grace and ease and for your highest good.

Give gratitude and affirm that the work has been done. Ring your bell or tingsha one more time here as a way of closing the ritual. Finally, open the front door to the house to allow all the negative energy to leave. Leave it open for five minutes or more. Leave the orange peels out for twenty-four hours to absorb any lingering negative energy. After a full day passes, throw them away or compost them.

BED SMACKING—
Space Cleansing for the Bed

We spend a third of our life in bed. This means our mattresses absorb everything we think and feel. Just as it is important to Space Clear your room, you need to Space Clear your mattress, using the same ingredients. In Fun Shway this is called Bed Smacking. It was inspired by a process called "bed thwacking" that I learned from master space clearer Karen Kingston in Bali, Indonesia.

1. First, **CALL IN THE LIGHT.** Here is a sample prayer you can use, and as always you can come up with your own if this one doesn't resonate. Ask the light to help you. "I ask you now to clear all low-vibrational energy, frustration, depression, confusion, lack of self-esteem, self-judgment, over-responsibility,

burden, grief, and anything and everything that is embedded into this mattress that no longer serves me or my highest and best good. I ask that it be released into the light and transmuted into love. I ask for this or something greater for my highest good. So it is."

2. Next, remove the sheets, pillowcases, and comforter and pound your fists on the mattress. Do this until you feel like all the old energy is out. I usually do it for five minutes.

3. Once this is finished, you can use incense or sage and waft it around the mattress. Make sure to have a bowl for your sage, so the sparks and ashes don't drop on your bed. Next, get your bowl with the orange peel.

4. Do the Om Mani Pad Mei Hum mantra with the Orange Peel Blessing (as described above).

5. Ring your bell or clap your hands over the mattress many times, until you feel that the energy that was released from the mattress has dissipated completely.

6. Next, lie down on the mattress. Recite this affirmation aloud (or use your own similar words): "This is a space for peace, rest, optimal health, and self-love."

7. Leave the peel for twenty-four hours and then throw it out or compost it.

Spend Some Time in Your
C.A.V.E.

CHAPTER 13

Spend Some Time in Your CAVE

Ready to be more creative? It's time to start building your CAVE, which stands for Creating Active Visual Energy. Don't worry, it's not a dark cave with cobwebs and creepy crawlers. It's the CAVE inside of you that you go into when you need some time to think, recharge, and access your imagination.

Your CAVE energizes you. It reminds you what is important in your life and what you want from it, and it helps you manifest it. While you turn your room into a container for blessings, it's equally important to make changes to your mental and emotional space: your CAVE. Fun Shway is all about the *Inner Shway* and the *Outer Shway*.

WRITE

Freewriting is a simple and fun way to get your worries, concerns, and upsets out of your system. Just ten minutes of writing will leave you feeling a lot better. It will release all that stored energy and make it easier to move about your day—and deal with your clutter. Just write down anything that comes to your mind. You might be surprised at the things going on in there.

Here's your first CAVE assignment:

Fun Shway Time

Use this space to write wildly and unabashedly. If you have more to say, then continue on another sheet of paper. Throw caution to the wind and just let yourself go, and most importantly, don't censor or think too much. If you need to keep going, then continue in your journal.

Once you are done writing, you can burn what you've written. It's up to you. The goal is to release that old crusty energy that is weighing you down. If something interesting came out of the writing, like a poem, just rewrite the poem on another sheet of paper and get rid of the rest. You don't want to hold that energy in your room or in your mind!

DRAW

Another way of releasing mental clutter is to draw. Sometimes if the words aren't there when I try writing, I turn to drawing. At one of the most hectic times in my life, I decided to pay a visit to my local drugstore. I bought a $2 sketch pad and a box of crayons. Every morning before getting out of bed or letting my mind wander into worry, I would pick up my pad and just draw everything I was feeling without censoring or judging myself. After five to ten minutes of scribbling and doodling, my attitude would shift from gloomy to grateful!

IMAGINE

When you devote fifteen minutes a day to aligning yourself with your heart's desire, then it's easier for the universe to know what you want and to deliver it to you. There is a saying: "If you can perceive it and believe it, then most surely you will achieve it." Esther Hicks, author of *Ask and It Is Given*, says that fifteen minutes of creative visualization a day can be like two thousand hours of action time.

I'm not saying that sitting and daydreaming all day will guarantee that everything will fall into your lap right away. Oh, how I wish! Creative visualization is different from daydreaming. What I am saying is that what you focus on expands. So, when you are consciously creating images in your mind, then those images start taking on a life of their own.

Being a dreamer gets a lot of bad press. I've been a huge dreamer for most of my life and I really believe it's what has ultimately helped me become a great visualizer. The difference between the two is that when you're daydreaming, you're kind of passively watching your fantasies. But when you're creatively visualizing, you're actively engaging your senses to create a real-life image of what your life could look like. You can see it, hear it, smell it, and sometimes even taste it, and all within your mind. It's well known that athletes, actors, and even politicians do it, and you can too!

BAGWHAATT?
The Nine Zones of Life

What if I could give you a road map that could help you make simple changes to your surroundings and give you significant results in your life? What if this map could guide you through your life, steer you safely in the right direction, and show you how to pave your own way? Well, there is one. It's called the Ba-Gua (pronounced "Ba-Gwa") and it's kind of like a navigational tool for bringing order to your room—and your mind. Think of it as a kind of GPS that will show you what areas of your life are the most blocked and in need of your attention.

Remember the number nine from chapter 12, and how I told you it was special? Well, here comes nine again! The Ba-Gua is a grid of nine zones. The zones relate to the most crucial elements of our lives: Prosperity, Wisdom, Health, Self-Image/Respect, Love, Family, Helpful People, Creativity, and Career. Using the Ba-Gua allows you to draw a grid over the top of your room and spot the areas that need the most work.

BAGWHAATT?
THE NINE ZONES OF LIFE

As you begin to look more closely at the areas that you most want to strengthen, you can refer to the Ba-Gua to introduce the right color, element, symbol, or words of wisdom that relate to that area of life into your room. In feng shui, these are called activators. They work by activating the Chi and redirecting the energy to create more harmony and flow. In Fun Shway, you will use activators to create positive change and new patterns in your environment.

Ba-Gua Map

Prosperity	Self Image	Love
 Appreciate what you have. Feel prosperous.	Know who you are. Celebrate your accomplishments.	Feel good about yourself. Surround yourself with people who love and support you.
Family  Harness healthy relationships with Mom, Dad, and your siblings!	Health Take great care of your body, mind, emotions, and spirit.	Creativity Express your inner artist. The world is your canvas— paint it!
Wisdom  Listen to your inner voice. Develop areas that you would like to improve.	Career & Life Path  What are your unique hobbies and talents?	Helpful People  Don't be afraid to ask for help. Ask and you shall receive. Your prayers will be heard!

By looking at your room from the perspective of the Ba-Gua you will be armed with a powerful tool to help you to live your life with intention!

Understanding these nine zones will help unblock the things that stand in your way and strengthen the areas you want to improve. Once you have superimposed the map on your room, find each life zone and pay attention to it.

When you feel something isn't working well in your life, you will find the corresponding section in your room and add an activator. Activators can be words, imagery, objects, the suggested color, shape, or the dominant element of the corresponding zone. Your intention is what ultimately activates the symbol you place in your room and will trigger attitudes that correspond to the quality of that symbol. Psychologist William James taught us that images, or mental pictures and ideas, produce the physical conditions and external acts that correspond to them.

Roberto Assagioli, a psychologist and student of Sigmund Freud (the father of modern psychology) said, "Holding new images before the eyes tends to produce the reality suggested by the image."

Many of your issues can be resolved using the map.

By giving attention to every zone, you will see how even in the smallest ways you can create more harmony and balance in your life. Since your bedroom is likely the one place you have the most control over, you'll probably want to start there. Later, if you choose to, you can superimpose this map over other parts of your house, your yard, and even your car.

As you learn more about each zone, you'll get better at finding the right activators. As my Feng Shui Master, Nate, says, "The best activators are the ones you come up with yourself."

Soon you are going to create a drawing of your bedroom from an aerial view and divide it into the nine zones. It's kind of like this:

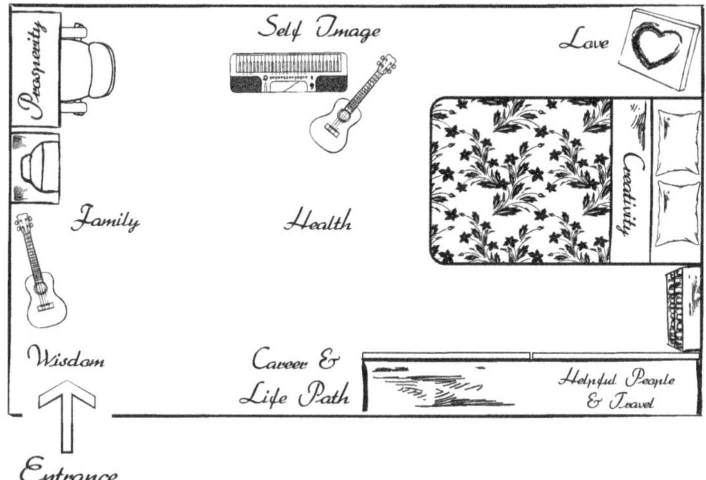

Draw Your Room

What you'll need:

* Ruler

* Pencil

* Eraser

* Paper (standard white 8½ x 11 or graph paper)

You don't need to be an architect or an artist to do this right. You'll just be sketching an outline of your bedroom and noting things like the door, the furniture, windows, and other angles of the room.

> 1. When you are ready, get a pencil and take out an 8½ x 11 piece of paper. Draw a picture of your bedroom from an aerial perspective—as if you are hovering above it, looking down at it like a bird would. Use the entire sheet of paper.

2. Draw your door, all the furniture, art, knick-knacks, the closet, and anything else that you think is important.

3. Now line it up with the Ba-Gua grid (which can be found on page 102) so that the front door lines up with the lower side of the Ba-Gua corresponding to *Wisdom, Career and Life Path*, or *Helpful People*. Then fill in the name of each zone: *Prosperity, Love, Creativity, Health, Family*, etc.

4. Examine the nine areas of your life and see if one or more of them needs your attention. You'll do this in greater detail in the next chapter. Whenever one area of our lives takes over, or one is not getting the TLC it needs, then we begin feeling drained, overwhelmed, and out of sorts.

5. Check which areas of your room are most cluttered and mark an X in the corresponding Ba-Gua zone. This is where you most likely have stagnant energy or Chi.

6. Remember those turbocharged affirmations you made? Now is the time to use them. Walk through your room, starting in the zone that most needs your attention, and say your affirmation out loud. You can also write it down. Place the affirmation in that section in a place that is either visible to you or hidden behind objects.

CHAPTER 15

Give Your Room a Voice

Are you not sure how you really feel about these different areas in your life? One great way to explore your grotto of feelings is to give each of the nine life zones in your room its own voice.

Dialoguing with your room can provide you with valuable information about how you truly feel. Giving the different areas in your room a voice is like role-playing. It's a powerful technique for tapping into your subconscious mind.

Did you ever role-play when you were a kid with your friends? Role-playing can sometimes bring to life feelings that have been hidden for a long time, so prepare yourself. Remember, you can do this when nobody's watching. Walk into each section and just imagine that it is alive and has a message for you.

EXAMPLE: "URGENT! YOU HAVE BEEN IGNORING ME FOR A WHILE NOW. CAN WE AT LEAST TALK ABOUT THIS?"

Give Your Room A Voice

Remember, the message can be anything about the physical space and/or about that part of your life. Most likely, it will be a combination of both. Like the other day, for example; I walked into the relationship corner of my room and listened to what it had to say to me. It said,

"YOU HAVE NEGLECTED ME AND NOW I'M A MESS! I WOULD LIKE TO SPEND MORE TIME IN NATURE WITH YOU."

As result, I scheduled a playdate with myself and went to the beach, and then I had the energy to clean up the corner.

What My Room is Trying to Tell Me:

Try this writing exercise to help yourself tap into your unconscious mind. Don't think. Just write the first thing that comes to mind.

Here are some writing prompts that will help you decode your room's secret language.

Room:

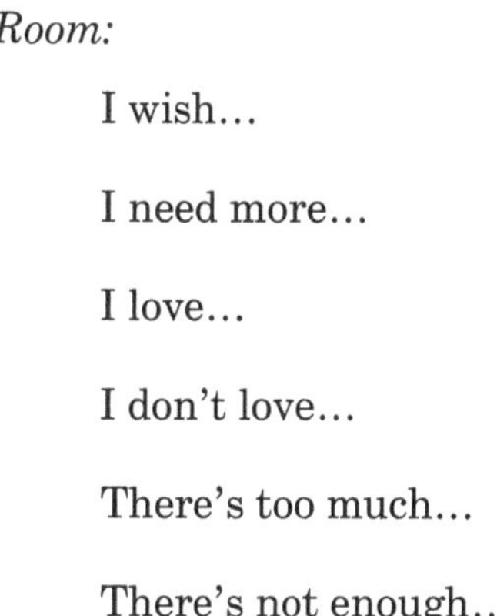

> I wish…
>
> I need more…
>
> I love…
>
> I don't love…
>
> There's too much…
>
> There's not enough…

Rate Your Room

Now that you have listened carefully to some of the things your room was trying to tell you, I would like you to bring your attention to the chart below where you will rate each area of your life. Rate the level of satisfaction on this scale of one to ten. You can even write inside the boxes.

RATING SCALE

1–4: "I am miserable and wish things could be different."

5–7: "I feel average and kind of apathetic." (an overall blah feeling, like you don't really care one way or another)

8–10: "I feel totally fulfilled. I love my life and feel satisfied with myself, like the universe is a friendly place to live."

Prosperity	Self / Image	Relationships & Love
Family	Health	Creativity
Wisdom	Career & Life Path	Helpful People/ Travel

The lower the number is on the scale of one to ten, the more this area of your life needs your love and attention. Pay specific attention to any areas you rated seven and lower.

In the chapters to come, you will learn both inner and outer activators for enhancing the different areas of your life.

By now you have a better sense of Fun Shway, and you get where all of this is going, and I think you are ready to look more closely at each of the nine zones of the Ba-Gua. As you look at each of these nine areas, we'll focus on the **Inner Shway,** the mental and emotional and spiritual work you do to help you function at your optimal level, and the **Outer Shway,** the physical expression of your inner experience, both in your room and in your life. These will always go together because the better you get at inner support, the more you will feel capable of going for what you want in the world.

As you move in and around the nine zones of the Ba-Gua, you will use the chart below as a guide for all the nine zones and their corresponding activators (i.e., elements, colors, shapes, numbers, and objects that are associated with those zones). Before you make major changes to your room, read the next chapters to form a deeper understanding of what each of these nine areas means.

Prosperity Color: Purple, Gold, Green Element: None Enhancers: Coins, piggy bank, pictures of what makes you feel abundant! Jewelry.	**Self Image** Color: Red, Green Element: Fire Destructive Element: Water Enhancers: Stars, shiny objects, headshot, candles, awards, red wall.	**Love** Color: Pink, White Element: None Enhancers: Objects in pairs, hearts, picture of your boy/girlfriend, happy people in love, symbols of love, roses, romantic poetry.
Family Color: Green, Black Element: Wood Destructive Element: Metal Enhancers: Plants, family pictures, heirlooms, pic of trees or the forest, wood objects.	**Health** Color: Yellow, Orange, Red Element: None Destructive Element: Wood Enhancers: Yoga mat, bright yellow bean bag, yellow square rug, ceramics.	**Creativity** Color: White, Yellow Element: Metal Destructive Element: Fire Enhancers: Art, music, bells, crafts, paint, instruments.
Wisdom Color: Blue Element: None Enhancers: Books, desk, scholastic awards, honors, degrees, pics of people you admire for their wisdom.	**Career & Life Path** Color: Black Helper Color: White Element: Water Destructive Element: Earth Enhancers: Water fountain, mirror, bells, Chimes, vision board of your ideal career.	**Helpful People** Color: Grey Element: None Enhancers: Symbols of places you want to travel, pictures of helpful people, religious objects, hands.

The placement of your door aligns with the lower grid of this map: Wisdom, Career & Life Path, or Helpful People

CHAPTER 16

Prosperity: Your Inner Riches

Inner Shway

When I was a teenager, my grandmother said, "You will never be poor because you are rich on the inside." At the time, I didn't really get what she meant. I assumed she meant I was a good person with a big heart. But her message was a lot deeper than what I could comprehend in that moment.

Imagine feeling rich for the rest of your life, no matter what. If I asked you right now what would make you feel prosperous, what would you say? Some of you might run off a list of things like an amazing wardrobe, a new bedroom set, the best makeup, cool jewelry, lots of new friends, love, infinite cash flow, a new car, or an amazing job.

PROSPERITY
Your Inner Riches

Here's the catch though: to feel prosperous for the rest of your life no matter what means letting go of the list. Does that sound counterintuitive? There's nothing wrong with having a list of nice things to aspire to. It's important to have goals. You should have seen my lists. They spanned entire journals!

But when feeling good inside hinges on having the items on the list, we run the risk of never truly experiencing our innate worthiness. We become dependent on having stuff to feel good about ourselves. In truth, what most people want is the emotional experience they associate with the items on their list.

All the great and wise sages have told us for eons that happiness is an inside job. By aligning your energy with the feelings that come from the things and experiences you want, the easier it will be for those things to find you.

Fun Shway Time

Identify what you most want right now. Then think: what is the experience I'm looking for? How will it make me feel once I get there?

Here are some examples.

I want: to travel to Paris for a month.

The experience I am looking for: to experience adventure and freedom.

I want: to lose weight and have an awesome new wardrobe.

The experience I am looking for: to feel secure in myself and feel fabulous.

I want: my parents to stop pressuring me.

The experience I am looking for: to feel approval and love.

I want: a romantic relationship.

The experience I'm looking for: to give and receive love.

Your Turn

I want:

. . . .

The experience I am looking for is:

. . . .

I want:

. . . .

The experience I am looking for is:

. . . .

I want:

. . . .

The experience I am looking for is:

. . . .

Once you identify the experience you're looking for, then you can call it in! For example, let's say you want a relationship, and the experience you are looking for is to feel loved and desired; you can use a turbocharged affirmation that you learned in chapter 9 and say, "I am grateful for the love I am receiving now. I deeply love myself exactly as I am. The right person recognizes my unique worth and value!"

When you get in touch with the experience you are seeking and affirm it, you naturally attract opportunities to have more of that experience. Give it a try!

Now that you have the inner foundation (Inner Shway) for prosperity, let's take this and anchor it into your room for some Outer Shway! The cool thing about Fun Shway is that we can use our rooms to reinforce the quality and experience we want to feel about ourselves.

Feng Shui is a symbolic language, so if something is broken, you may be feeling very broke or broken, too.

Prosperity

Outer Shway

Fun Shwaying the Prosperity Zone of your room helps you

* Save money for a special trip or gift

* Feel deserving of receiving what you wish for

* Set yourself up for success in your life

* Create an abundance frame of mind

* Get a pay raise or promotion at work

Prosperity

Color: Purple, Gold, Green
Element: None
Enhancers: Coins, piggy bank, plants, jewelry; pictures of what makes you feel abundant!
Body Part: Hip
Number: 8

Purple is the color that activates the prosperity section. Historically, it has been associated with royalty. Purple fabric was so expensive that only kings and queens could afford it.

You can either place purple here or something else that makes you feel opulent. Prosperity means having more than enough, being in the overflow, having so much that you feel generous.

Determine what prosperity feels like to you and bring those symbols into this section of your room. What imagery makes you feel prosperous? For me, it's gold, nature, beautiful luxurious fabrics, places I want to visit, items with bling, and images of people who have achieved the success I want.

Fun Shway Prosperity Activators:

* Anything in purple—pillows, blankets, wallpaper, a chair painted purple

* All your Lovable and most cherished items

* Shiny objects and light-refracting or moving objects like crystals and wind mobiles hung from the ceiling that call in wealth and prosperity

* Your wish list for super fab gifts you want to receive

* Your piggy bank (start saving for that trip to Paris with your friends!)

* Posters, paintings, collages, or pictures of things you'd like to buy or experience

* Your favorite quotes and sayings relating to abundance, riches, and gratitude hung or placed here

Fun Shway Prosperity Blockers:

* Keep your garbage can out of this section or put a lid on it so it doesn't catch your good Chi!

* Too many candles will burn up your money and your mojo.

* Images of poverty, loneliness, and barren landscapes don't belong here!

* Any clutter or too much stuff in a tiny space chokes money.

* Items that are broken or torn.

*   If your toilet is here, you may be flushing away your riches. Make sure to always keep the lid down and hang a multifaceted crystal over the toilet, or a picture of a tree or a mountain on the wall behind the toilet to keep your Chi elevated.

SUCCESS STORY

During a feng shui session with Ana, a very talented singer/songwriter, I noticed an old broken ukulele hanging over her bed in the prosperity section of her room. She said, "I'm always broke and can't make a living as a singer." Her dream was to get her songs produced, but her intention was being thwarted by the message that this broken object was sending. The broken ukulele reinforced her feeling of being broke. Once she took it down and replaced it with a new ukulele, her energy changed, and so did her luck. The last time we spoke, she had released her first album.

CHAPTER 17

Self-Image & Power: Who Do You Think You Are?

Inner Shway

Some of us (myself included) have at some point in our lives suffered from starstruck-ness, or as I like to refer to it, starSTUCK-ness. I thought celebrities were a special breed who have the proverbial "it factor"—genius, talent, and discipline beyond anything I could ever have. I compared myself to those I admired, never feeling I measured up, and as a result my self-image suffered. Unfortunately, this type of thinking made it difficult for me to identify my own unique talents and gifts.

Self-Image & Power

Who Do You Think You Are?

Working in casting for film and television in Hollywood has shown me that celebrities, despite their status, are just as prone to self-comparison. Yet what stands out is their mutual celebration of greatness, including their own. Think about it: the definition of celebrity is 'the state of being celebrated.' It's like a collective recognition of each other's unique contributions — the Oscars exemplify this!

Consider this: being celebrated starts with celebrating yourself and recognizing the greatness in others — qualities you likely share.

When you can see the greatness in someone else and you're having trouble seeing it in yourself, it's called a Positive Projection. But here's the bottom line: you couldn't see someone else's beauty, talent, and confidence if you didn't have it within yourself. One of the most valuable lessons I'm learning daily is how to own my Positive Projections and realize that the qualities I admire in other people, I also possess.

Fun Shway Time

Owning Positive Projections

Think of people who you highly admire and who possess the qualities that you wish you had. Here are a few examples of my own:

> **Jennifer:** She is confident and successful, and she has the devotion and commitment to finish what she starts.

> **Oprah:** She does lots of great things to help humanity. She has so much self-respect—and millions of women around the world respect her, too.

> **Alexis:** She is calm and peaceful and maintains her composure even under pressure.

List five people you admire and what qualities make them admirable to you.

1.

....

2.

....

3.

....

4.

....

5.

....

Now that you've identified these people and their outstanding qualities, I encourage you to go over the list and find where you have exhibited the same or similar qualities in your own life. A big part of growing your self-worth and value happens by owning those Positive Projections and acknowledging yourself!

For example:

1. Even though it took me over a decade, I had the commitment and devotion to complete Fun Shway.

2. I love helping my family, friends and clients live their best life.

3. I was composed while receiving constructive feedback from my partner today.

Your Turn

1.

....

2.

....

3.

. . . .

4.

. . . .

Can you see how you have those things inside you already? There is always room to grow, but it's easier to grow from a positive starting point than a negative one.

Let's continue building your positive self-image. Identify five qualities that you really like about yourself. These may or may not be things that other people know about you. Here are some examples:

> 1. I have a great sense of humor and make my friends laugh.

> 2. I am generous and I share my gifts with my family and friends.

> 3. I am intuitive and am blessed with a strong inner vision.

> 4. I am creative and I come up with the most incredible ideas!

> 5. I am an inspiration to myself and others.

Your Turn

1.

....

2.

....

3.

....

4.

....

5.

....

Remember, writing down these positive affirmations can help anchor them deeper into your subconscious mind until it becomes a part of your belief system. Now that you have the inner foundation (Inner Shway) for Self-Image and Power, let's anchor it into your room for some Outer Shway.

Self-Image & Power

Outer Shway

Fun Shway this part of your room when you want to:

- Receive credit/ recognition for your hard work

- Increase your confidence

- Establish a good reputation

- Gain more respect

- Step into a new image of yourself

- Shine

Power/Self-Image

Color: Red, Green
Element: Fire
Destructive Element: Water
Enhancers: Stars, shiny objects, headshot, candles, awards, red wall
Body Part: Eye
Number: 1

What are you good at? Is there anything you want the world to know about you, but you've been too shy to share? Is there a secret talent or something you've always wanted to explore, but haven't had the guts to? Put it here. You'll get used to looking at it and eventually, you'll be courageous enough to share it with others. Don't be afraid to sparkle and flare! Show your best self in this area of your room by sharing your accomplishments and the things you are proud of!

Fun Shway Self-Image and Power Activators:

* All colors in the family of red.

* If your bed is here, dress up with a coral throw or pillow as accents.

* If you can paint the wall, stencil some words that represent or show how you want to be seen by the world in a shade of red.

* Things that come to a point such as stars and suns and pyramids, candles, fire, or pictures of these things.

* If you want to be recognized for your achievements, then put your name on a star and place it up high on the wall—or let it hang from the ceiling!

* Sunflowers represent the fire element and make a great addition to this area.

* Symbols of your accomplishments like awards, trophies, honors, and diplomas.

* Favorite sayings from people who inspire you and who you would like to emulate in the future.

* Pictures of people who have accomplished some of your dreams.

* A picture of you at your best! If you're wearing red, it's an extra Chi lift!

* Symbols of your goals for the future.

* A vision board of people who have achieved some of your greatest wishes and desires.

* What do you want to be famous for? Write it down on red paper and hang it up here!

* Place a cactus in this area when you need to ward off some nasty rumors or gossip coming your way.

Fun Shway Self-Image and Power Blockers:

* Blue.

* Water or images of water (puts out the fire!).

* Ovals and circles.

* Water bottles drown the flames.

* Fish tanks will put out the fire.

* Mirrors create too much water energy.

* Pictures of people you don't respect or admire. People that only have the cool actor vibe and nothing else remarkable about them. Cool freezes and you want to light up the world with all of who you are!

SUCCESS STORY

I moved to Los Angeles from Seattle to pursue a career in casting for film and TV. After months of sending resumes and making calls to no avail, I realized I needed some help. Then I met a helpful person. He was an actor and a feng shui consultant. He gave me my first book on feng shui. One of the assignments was to make a vision board. I included a picture of myself in the center and names of casting directors orbiting around me. I wrote down on the bottom of the board my affirmation: "The right casting direc-tor hires me for a full-time job in casting." Then I placed a red candle to symbolize my energy going out to the world and getting recognized as the right person for the job. A few days later I got a call for an interview; the next day I was offered my first job in Hollywood! I am my first feng shui success story.

THE HEALTH AND HEALING ZONE
health

CHAPTER 18

The Health and Healing Zone

Inner Shway

The zone that corresponds to health and healing is always smack dab in the center of your bedroom. Can you guess why it's the only area in the Ba-Gua that touches all the others? When your health gets compromised, so does everything else.

You might be thinking, "I'm young. I don't need to worry about my health just yet." When you're young and feeling good, it's easy to take for granted the amazing gift of health. But, if you don't tend to the garden of your body, mind, and spirit, then your good health will dwindle. Poor health can take heaps of time, money, and energy to repair. So, start early and create healthy habits that will last a lifetime.

During my teens and early twenties, I didn't know how to deal with my insecurities, so I ate my way into numbness. I remember one time when I was fifteen, I was home sick from school and I devoured a two-and-a-half-pound bag of gummy bears! Back then I couldn't see that I was just stuffing my sad feelings down with food, or that this behavior was only going to offer temporary relief from whatever I didn't want to feel. When we resist our feelings, they stick around. When you push your emotions down with food, or anything else addictive, you become numb and feel worse later. "E-motions" are energy in motion. That means you've got to feel them to heal them.

I didn't know that I could stop and pay attention to what I was feeling inside, and that would offer relief, so instead I pushed my emotions down with food. Now I understand that all feelings are there because they are meant to be felt. I try to be mindful about what's motivating my food choices. Ask yourself: "Am I eating out of hunger, or because I don't want to feel some uncomfortable sensation that's coming up?"

Now is the time to welcome all feelings! This may seem like a strange concept. Especially if you've bottled up your feelings for a long time, like I did. The trick is to let go. If you just welcome them and feel without judgment, they will pass. Sometimes, if you've held things in for a long time, it may take a couple of hours or days to do this. If you don't have a day, then just do what you can to honor your feelings in the moment.

One of my favorite affirmations to welcome my feelings is:

IT IS SAFE FOR ME TO FEEL ALL MY FEELINGS. I ALLOW ALL MY FEELINGS TO FLOW WITH EASE AND GRACE.

Food for thought: Studies show that a combination of unhealthy emotional overeating patterns can literally bankrupt your diet. Binge eating usually involves eating unhealthy things. When you're binging, you're looking for the closest thing to mask your emotions. That's why they call it "fast food." It's the food that doesn't require much preparation, like candy bars, chips, sweetened breakfast cereals, fruit juices, pastries, cookies and cakes, etc. Most things that come in a bag or box lack enough vitamins and mineral enzymes to meet your body's nutritional needs. You're not just stuffing down your feelings, you're also robbing your body of what it needs to function well and feel good. It's a strange thought that someone can be ten to sixty pounds overweight and still be nutritionally bankrupt. Eating a lot doesn't mean your body is getting the nutritionally dense foods you need to thrive!

Fun Shway Time

1. Keeping a feeling/food journal can support you in honestly examining some of the choices you are making. Give yourself twenty minutes each night before you go to bed to jot down what you ate that day, your feelings prior to putting it in your mouth, and how it made you feel afterward. Track your energy levels too. Notice the foods that contribute to feelings of sleepiness and fatigue, and the ones that made you feel light and energized. Be honest with yourself about your eating habits. You will see the correlation between your moods and everything you put in your mouth. If you're feeling sad on a particular day, give yourself some "soul nourishment" (see below for tips) before turning to something that will take the edge off at the moment but leave you feeling crappy later.

2. "Soul nourishment" helps soothe emotions and will curb your urge to binge or grab something with little or no nutritional value. A loving hug, a belly rub, a positive affirmation are great ways to soothe a sad mood. Give your body the love and attention it deserves. Take a warm bath or get a massage. Look in the mirror and tell your body how grateful you are for everything it does for you.

The Health and Healing Zone

Outer Shway

Fun Shway this section of your room when you want to:

- Lose a couple of pounds
- Eat healthier and make better nutritional choices
- Stop emotional overeating
- Feel better about your body image
- Get more rest, rejuvenation, and exercise

Health

Color: Yellow, Red
Element: Earth
Destructive Element: Wood
Enhancers: Yoga mat, bright yellow bean bag, yellow square rug, ceramics
Body Part: All not mentioned.
Number: 9

* Get un-stuck from negative thoughts and change your attitude

* Live a more balanced, harmonious, stress-free life

* Make more self-honoring choices and take excellent care of yourself physically, emotionally, and spiritually

The way to utilize the health section of your room is to first check out what's in the center of your room! This area reflects the state of your health, so keep it clean. If your bed is here, then look at what you are stashing under the bed. Place a yoga mat for stretching, or even a cushion for meditation. Make a health box to store clippings and info you find about health and healing. The health section touches every other area of the room, so making health enhancements in any area will help.

Fun Shway Health Activators:

* Anything that is square, earthy, or yellow.

* Bright and happy stuff like sunflowers.

* A yellow or orange yoga mat, or any yoga mat! Stretch, jump, and downward dog here!

* Keep your (nurturing) journal here. Fill it with everything you find healthy for your mind, body, and soul.

* Keep magazine images depicting what "ideal health" means to you.

* Cut out three yellow circles and place them here. They don't have to be visible to anyone but you.

Fun Shway Health Blockers:

* No plants or anything from wood. This uproots the earth energy of this area.

* Water fountains and anything water, like a blue rug, can make you feel sappy or lethargic.

* No junk food whatsoever should be here.

* Please avoid keeping magazines featuring heavily photoshopped or unrealistically skinny models here. Many of those women you see in fashion magazines have unhealthy relationships with their bodies and deprive themselves of the food they need. Being skinny doesn't guarantee happiness, so look for images of women who have realistic-looking bodies and look healthy and happy.

SUCCESS STORY

Alex was nineteen and feeling more depressed by the day. She stopped playing her piano, wasn't really interested in spending time with her friends, and spent most of her time with her boyfriend. She was fed up and felt like things between them were stagnating. When I walked into her room, the first thing I noticed was that she still had many toys from early childhood and her tween years. Her room was frozen in time. She shared that she hadn't felt happy since her younger years. Then I discovered that Alex was sleeping on a mattress pad in the Health and Healing zone of her room. It belonged to her deceased grandma, who had a history of mental illness. I immediately instructed her to throw it away. That was the first step. Next, she said goodbye to her fuzzy childhood friends. What followed was a full-blown transformation. Soon thereafter, Alex's mood improved drastically, she let go of the boyfriend, and ended up meeting a great guy who was a musician. Through his encouragement, she got back into her music and found her way back into her power. You can read more about Alex's success story in the appendix where I present case studies.

CAREER & LIFE PURPOSE
What's Calling You?

CHAPTER 19

Career and Life Purpose: What's Calling You?

Inner Shway

"What do you want to be when you grow up?" Like nearly every teenager, I was asked this question a thousand times. When I was a kid, I would play doctor and operate on my Barbie dolls. My parents would look at me fondly and say, "Look, she's going to be a surgeon!" Then at the age of twelve, I was hooked on *Perry Mason*, a TV show about a trial attorney. My parents would smile with pride and say to their friends, "She's going to be a lawyer." Then at the age of twenty-one when I wasn't really showing any interest in law or medicine, my parents said, "I guess she is going to marry a doctor or a lawyer." Then, in my late twenties, I told my parents I was going to be a feng shui practitioner. My dad said, "What kind of sushi is that?" It took them a decade to warm up to feng shui, let alone pronounce it.

After graduating from college, some strive for a career that society, or their parents, tells them will bring them the most money and security, while others figure out how to make money doing what they love. But the latter is not the norm, and figuring out what you love can take time.

Statistics show that many people change their careers at least seven times in a lifetime! As we evolve, so do our values and priorities, our likes and dislikes. The jobs we want when we're twenty may not be the ones that appeal to us in our thirties or forties.

There is a well-known period in a young adult's life called the quarter-life crisis. It's kind of like a midlife crisis, only it happens between the ages of twenty-five and thirty-two, and earlier for some. It's a period of uncertainty where you review your life choices and reevaluate the direction of your life. During this time, many find themselves feeling burned out and dissatisfied with their jobs; they venture out in search of something more meaningful—a career that will give their life purpose and fulfillment.

A life's purpose combines your talents and skills and usually serves a larger purpose than that of simply making you money. Although wealth can be a byproduct, it's not the sole aim.

A life purpose:

* Allows you to use your natural gifts, talents, and abilities.

* Stretches your comfort zone and promotes growth and learning.

* Contributes to the world.

* Provides financial stability.

Knowing yourself is a major step in the process of finding out what you're here to do. Don't worry; you don't need to have it all figured out right now. Open your mind to a vision of the future—one where you are deeply satisfied and thriving, even if it changes along the way.

You can start by answering these questions:

1. What are my natural gifts?

2. What comes easily for me?

3. If I had all the money in the world, what would I do with my time?

4. What are the things I do for hours that make me lose track of time?

5. Is there a voice in my head that keeps urging me to try something, but I think of every excuse in the book for why I can't? What is it?

Your Turn

Define the qualities that are most important for you to experience in a job.

Fun Shway Time

Envisioning Your Purpose

Set aside some quiet time when you know you won't be interrupted to do this exercise:

1. Close your eyes.

2. Relax all the muscles in your body.

3. Take three deep breaths in through your nose and breathe out of your mouth.

4. Once you are completely relaxed, invite your higher self forward—the part that can see into the future and know the larger picture of your purpose on this planet.

5. Ask that it show you an image of yourself in the future. Let go of trying to figure anything out. Just allow yourself to receive an image.

6. Once you have received the vision or a feeling, write it down here in as much detail as possible.

Career & Life Purpose

Outer Shway

Fun Shway this part of your room when:

* You're looking for a job

* You're exploring a career track

* You are looking for your place in the world

* There is a certain job you want to land

* You want to create more job opportunities

* You want a promotion in your current job

* Before you have an important job interview

Career & Life Purpose

Color: Black
Helper Color: White
Element: Water
Destructive Element: Earth
Enhancers: Water fountain, mirror, bells, chimes, vision board of your ideal career
Body Part: Ear
Number: 6

This part of your room has to do with the color black and the element of water. If you want some extra help to determine your life purpose you can try this water technique developed by Jose Silva. It's kind of like a shortcut to connecting to your higher self and getting a vision for what your life path looks like. Water is also the dominant element for this section and can really contribute to the power of this exercise.

Do this water technique exercise right before bedtime:

> Get a full glass of water.

> Wrap both hands around the glass but make sure that your fingertips aren't touching.

> Close your eyes, roll your eyeballs back in your head, and think of your question, like "What does my life purpose or career look like," or "What is the next step in the right direction of my calling?"

> Then say inwardly, "This is all I need to do to solve the problem in my mind."

> Drink half of the cup and leave it in the "career" section of your room overnight. First thing upon rising in the morning, repeat the exercise, drinking the rest of the water. You may receive an answer in your dreams. If not, then pay attention to signs throughout your day, like a song that comes on, or a repetitive feeling you get, or a billboard you see that catches your attention. I have done this exercise several times and it has never failed me.

Fun Shway Career & Life Path Activators:

* All shades of black and indigo blue.

* Real water, such as a water fountain, or pictures of water.

* Mirrors represent the water element and are great here.

* Affirmations relating to following your dreams and living your purpose.

* Symbols, books, or any items that depict the career of your dreams.

* References to the job you're in now and the one you want to be in.

* A simple glass or vase with fresh water and some flowers.

* Start a career wish list where you write down the careers that sound interesting that you may want to explore and research later.

* Images of people in careers you think are cool.

Fun Shway Career & Life Path Blockers:

* Yellow (because yellow represents the earth element, and earth dams water).

* Junk or broken items (make you feel like something isn't working).

* Incomplete projects.

* Old clothes that you never wear (keep you stuck in an older version of yourself).

* Ceramics and earth elements. These will dam the water that presides over this section.

* Pictures of people that are not pursuing their dreams or in careers you don't want to explore.

SUCCESS STORY

Ricky, a commercial actor and painter in Los Angeles, asked me to help him feng shui his space for success. His real dream was to share his message, which was that everyone is creative, with the world. He needed to manifest enough money that he could devote the rest of his time to painting and to outreach work in the community to get his message out. We placed a fountain in the career section of his room, which is governed by the element of water. We gave the water an intention and told it to open the floodgates of abundance. The following week he landed a national commercial and was paid $20,000 plus residuals. That gave him enough money to subsidize the rest of the year and focus on what he really wanted, which was to keep painting and create opportunities for people of all ages to paint.

CHAPTER 20

Family Harmony: Feel to Heal

Inner Shway

You know the people that we love and can't stand at the same time, the people we wish would just leave us alone, and the ones we wish were paying more attention to us? These are the people we call family. These are the people that point out our flaws and, hopefully, encourage our strengths. Sometimes they are just exactly what we need, and sometimes, well… not.

Growing up I wished my parents could be like my best friend's parents who seemed so upbeat, positive, and approving of her choices. They seemed to be the perfect family. I would ask God every night why I couldn't have parents like those. As it turned out, my friend's family, like every other family, had their unique flaws. Until I learned to accept and appreciate the family I was born into, I couldn't find peace in my life. The process of love and acceptance didn't just happen overnight. First, I allowed myself to feel all the emotions I had stuffed down for so long, such as frustration, disappointment, anger, and sadness.

Family Harmony
Feel to Heal

Next, I had to let go of the expectation that my parents would change or that I could change them. I sent love, light, and forgiveness to those places inside of me that hurt and desperately needed something from them that they couldn't give me. I became a parent to myself by developing a loving inner dialogue with myself.

Once I was able to love and accept myself more fully, it was easier to open my heart and love my parents exactly as they were without expecting them to change. I came to the realization that even though my parents weren't capable of meeting many of my emotional needs in the way I needed them to, they were doing the best job they could.

When I changed my inner relationship with my mom and dad, our external relationship took a major turn for the better. It keeps getting better and better every day. You, too, can improve your inner relationships with the people you are close to. After all, happiness is an inside job.

Fun Shway Time: Forgiveness

One of the most valuable practices I learned at the University of Santa Monica's spiritual psychology program was self-forgiveness. We accumulate emotional baggage when we don't let go of the pain from the past and carry it with us indefinitely. Letting go of old hurts and releasing yourself from any pain or judgments you've made against yourself and your family is one of the most vital things you could ever do. When you forgive the judgment, it creates more space for feeling and healing. Try this exercise to practice self-forgiveness:

Put your hand on your heart and repeat these statements (out loud or silently) to yourself. If emotions start bubbling up just say yes to them and let them pass:

I forgive myself for judging myself as

. . . .

I forgive myself for judging my mom and dad as

. . . .

I forgive myself for buying into the belief that

. . . .

The truth about me and my family is

. . . .

Family Harmony Zone

Outer Shway

Fun Shway this section of your room when:

* You are fighting with your family and want to resolve misunderstandings or miscommunications

* You are feeling misunderstood by your parents

* You've got a bad case of sibling rivalry

* You want to spend more quality time with your loved ones

* You feel like you just aren't being heard

* You want to receive your family's support for something

* You want to heal something from the past

Family Harmony Zone

Color: Green, Black
Element: Wood
Destructive Element: Metal
Enhancers: Plants, family pictures, heirlooms, pic of trees or the forest, wood objects
Body Part: Foot
Number: 4

Do you still have lots of old pictures and stuff you associate with the not-so-good times? Remember, your room is either giving you energy or depleting it. All belongings are chatty. Pictures you associate with an unhealthy or unhappy time in your life can drain you. You don't have to throw things away that have negative memories. When you have forgiven and overcome any minor tragedy in your life, then you can bless the object by saying a little prayer over it.

Try this: Imagine white light filling the object or picture. The white light will dissolve some of the old energy around it. If you're still in the recovery zone, then I would say just take the good memories and let that object go because whether you look at it or not, it affects you.

Are there members of the family that you're struggling with? Is there a long-overdue conversation that needs to happen? Use this area to improve your relationships with members of your family. Connecting with family is like getting back in touch with the roots of yourself. Put a picture of your mom or dad or sibling here as a first step to reaching out.

This area has to do with the wood element and the color green. Some of the greatest cures for the family section of my life I have found on my walks out in nature. Just a short breezy walk around the trails can refresh your mind. Those moments of clear thinking can offer the solution to many problems. Nature has a way of clearing out the mind and putting you back in touch with what's important. And it is one of the greatest stress relievers.

Are you spending enough time in nature? Go for a walk and bring back a gift from mother earth and put it into this section. This is one of the best ways to gather positive Chi for your Family Harmony Zone.

Fun Shway Family Activators:

* Wood/green/rectangular objects.

* Family heirlooms.

* Healthy plants with rounded leaves.

* Anything made from wood.

* Pictures of Mom and Dad or anyone in your family.

* A list of how you want to be treated and how you will treat others in your household.

* Quotes related to forgiveness, security, and support.

* Cut a circle out of yellow construction paper and place a picture of the person you want to heal your relationship with (remember yellow corresponds with the Health and Healing Zone).

Fun Shway Family Blockers:

* Keep metal and white out of this area—it will chop up the wood.

* Too much fire will also burn up the wood, so reduce the color red, as well as candles and pointy objects.

* Any object or image that takes you back to an unhappy time in your life.

* Dead plants.

* Pictures of people who don't really support you and that you no longer want to engage with.

SUCCESS STORY

Jackie wanted to improve her relationship with her younger sister. They were very different, and the differences of opinion often ended in big fights. I suggested she find a picture of the two of them from a time when they were getting along. She picked one from a trip they took a few years back. I instructed her to draw a heart around both and on the back of the picture write this phrase: "I'm sorry. Please forgive me. Thank you. I love you." I then told her to place the photo in the Family Zone of her room with the intention to heal the relationship.

I said, "Every time you think of your sister in a negative way, repeat those words." As I explained to Jackie, these words come from a Hawaiian practice called **Ho'oponopono** and contain healing energies of reconciliation and forgiveness. A few weeks after following my guidance Jackie shared that she and her sister were getting along better than ever.

CHAPTER 21

Relationships: True Love Starts with Self-Love

Inner Shway

The people who show up in our lives—the wonderful, brilliant, and cruel—act as a mirror for us. If you're impatient, judgmental, or critical with yourself, then don't be surprised if that's what shows up in your relationships, too. The good news is that you can do something about it by learning how to strengthen your "self-honoring muscle." Like any muscle, it will go weak if you don't use it.

Let me tell you a little about Janet, who came to one of my workshops. She wanted a boyfriend who would love and appreciate her just the way she was. She said that the last one called her fat. I could see there was a lot of pain in her eyes as she shared with the group. When I asked her how she felt about her body, she said,

RELATIONSHIPS
TRUE
Love
starts with
self-love

"I don't like it very much. I really need to lose weight." There it was. The men she attracted reflected her own insecurities about her body. The first step was to practice unconditional love and appreciation. She had to learn to appreciate herself despite her perceived "flaws" and do it consistently.

Janet went to work in the self-love department. She started to observe the negative voices inside and the pain her own thoughts were causing. Little by little, she learned to stop listening to the critical part and to affirm her inner and outer beauty. It wasn't an instant success, but she kept at it, learning to appreciate her body and see herself through loving eyes. She strengthened her self-honoring muscle. A few months later, she met an amazing guy who loves and appreciates her just as she is.

Romance

Being in a relationship can be one of the greatest teachers in the universe. There is so much you can learn about yourself and others. Relationships teach us about the parts of ourselves we like and don't like, as well as what we want and don't want in a partner. Whether you're in a romantic relationship right now but are kind of struggling, or are ready to attract one, the first thing you can do to prepare is to release the ex memorabilia.

I'm not saying you need to "hex your ex." Just take him or her out of your bedroom. Holding onto gifts from an old relationship signifies that you are not ready for someone new. So, clear out the poetry, gifts, love notes, and pictures of your ex. If you're still sleeping with the teddy bear they bought you for Valentine's Day, or still have their clothes stashed under your bed, it's time to make them disappear.

If you're holding onto their stuff, some part of you isn't totally available for love. Check for other ways you might be showing up as "unavailable" in your bedroom. Is your room an homage to Harry Styles? Not only is it highly unlikely you'll end up his darling no matter how much creative visualization you do, but having him on your wall might send the wrong message to the universe. Also, make sure that the Relationship Zone of your room (the far right-hand corner from the door) is symbolic of the love you want. In the next section on the **Relationship Zone,** you'll do an inquiry and check for anything that could be potentially zapping the romance out of your life.

Fun Shway Time

There are two parts to attracting the right relationship. First, you'll want to figure out what your emotional needs are. It's easier to recognize the right person when you've identified what it is that you're looking for.

Example:

Someone to love me exactly as I am.

Someone whom I can trust.

Someone who will make me feel beautiful.

Someone who is faithful and keeps their word.

Someone who is social and likes to go out.

Someone who is driven and ambitious.

Someone who shares my family values.

Someone who listens and gives constructive feedback.

Your Turn

1.

. . . .

2.

. . . .

3.

. . . .

4.

. . . .

Although it would be a miracle to meet someone who could fulfill all your needs, the truth is that you can't expect someone else to do all the work for you. First, it would place too much pressure on the relationship. Second, even if they wanted to, somewhere along the way they may fail, because there are places inside of you that only you can reach.

When you identify your own needs and start to meet them in small and large ways, you will feel so full that it will be impossible to stop love from finding you! One small way to start this process is to use affirmations to reinforce your intentions. As many people know, where intention goes, energy flows.

Example:

* I love myself exactly as I am.

* I approve of me.

* I can trust myself.

* I am beautiful inside and out.

* I am faithful and true to my word.

* I create time for friends.

* I am excited about my dreams and take action to achieve them.

* Family is important and I make the time to nurture those relationships.

Your Turn

1.

....

2.

....

3.

....

4.

....

Relationships Zone

Outer Shway

Fun Shway this area of your room when you want to:

* Feel good about yourself

* Attract friends who love and support you as you are

* Increase feelings of self-worth and self-acceptance

* Attract the right partner who will appreciate you

> **Relationships Zone**
>
> **Color:** Pink, White
> **Element:** None
> **Enhancers:** Objects in pairs like hearts and candles, picture of your boy/girlfriend, happy people in love, symbols of love, roses, romantic poetry
> **Body Part:** All major organs
> **Number:** 2

The Relationship Zone lives in the far-right corner of your room. Make sure it's always clean and tidy and that everything works. Look out for reminders of a broken heart, or a friendship that went awry. Do an inquiry and check for anything that could be potentially zapping the romance out of your life, like images of single people, broken items, or too many "onesies"—things all by themselves, like one flower, candle, stone, a lonely crystal or pen, etc.

A powerful spiritual tool for calling in the right companion is a love-manifesting altar. This anchors your heart's desire and helps you become clear and specific about what you want. Start by finding a place in your room dedicated for your altar that only you can see. Next, collect items that resonate with your vision for romance and love, such as postcards, magazine clippings, stones, love quotes, and anything that makes you melt. If you need inspiration, use the suggestions from the Relationship Activators below.

Fun Shway Relationship Activators:

* Pink, red, and white things.

* Candles, hearts, statues.

* Essential oils of rose, frankincense, vanilla, and sandalwood.

* Pictures of your friends and boyfriend or girlfriend.

* Introduce symbols and artwork depicting love, equality, and harmony.

* Make a list of the qualities you want in a friend, boyfriend, or girlfriend, and put it here in a heart-shaped box.

* Write the kind of love letters you want to receive from someone or write one to yourself and place it here; read it often.

* Make room on both sides of the bed to invite romance.

Fun Shway Relationship Blockers:

* ✳ Ex memorabilia.

* ✳ Pictures of single women or men.

* ✳ Girly, pink, and frilly stuff everywhere.

* ✳ For guys, having too many "guy" symbols, like walls covered with sports heroes, cars, and guy stuff; this can hold your single status in place.

* ✳ Too many stuffed animals and toys that might keep you stuck in your childhood.

* ✳ Pictures of people who are no longer your friends.

* ✳ Dying plants.

* ✳ Dry flowers.

* ✳ Anything broken.

A NOT-SO-SUCCESSFUL STORY

Sometimes, I like to illustrate what happens when we don't make changes and stay the same. In this story, Liz had an album in her closet full of special moments—pictures, postcards, and love letters—from a relationship that had ended several years prior. The relationship was incredibly toxic, but she was unwilling to let go of the memorabilia.

On some level, Liz didn't trust that it was possible to have a healthy, mutually uplifting relationship, so she clung to her ex's memory. She was anchored to the past and not yet ready to call forward the best possible partner.

I suggested she look at each photo and express gratitude for the good times, and then burn or send them into the ocean, symbolically letting go of that which no longer served her. But she never took my advice. Seven years later, she reunited with the same guy. He told her he'd changed, and she believed him. They had a whirlwind romance, and he quickly proposed. Within a year of their marriage, she realized that nothing had changed. He was the same guy—only worse. Keeping relics from the past represented her reluctance to fully let go and held her back from healing, growing, and being available for the right person to find her. Luckily, she got right back on track and has since moved on from that experience and released the photos!

CHAPTER 22

Knowledge & Wisdom: Tune In to Your Knowing

Inner Shway

Are you amazing at giving your friends advice, but when it comes to helping yourself, you stare up at the ceiling in a daze? It's often hard to step back and look at our own problems objectively. This section is intended to help you develop the skills to be your own best adviser.

Did you know that infinite wisdom and insight are available to you anytime? There is a wise person inside of you right now that has the answers to your questions and can help you gain insight into your problems. Our wisdom helps us determine if we are ready to enter an intimate relationship or not, and with whom to be vulnerable or cautious.

Knowledge & Wisdom
TUNE IN TO YOUR KNOWING

But first, you need to ask.

Your inner wisdom doesn't always respond in a booming voice that you can hear. It's important to remember that inner guidance comes in many forms: creative ideas, insights in a dream, hunches, gut feelings, intuitive knowing, and premonitions.

If you haven't been following your inner wisdom, it may have gone on hiatus for a while. The good news is that you can always bring it back. It's important to set aside some time for tuning back in. Keep a journal and track each time you get a hunch. Write down your results. Name the positive experiences you have when you follow your inner wisdom, and what happens when you don't. This will help build confidence in your inner wisdom.

Fun Shway Time

A Letter to Your Wise Inner Self

On the next page, write a letter to your wise inner self. Begin with "Dear Wisdom." Then write about a difficult situation that you are going through and need guidance with. Give voice to all your feelings. Don't hold back. End the letter by saying, "Please, write through my pen. Thank you very much." Then write a letter back to yourself from the voice of your inner wisdom. Use a personal journal if you need more space to continue this exercise.

Dear Wisdom,

Please, write through my pen.
Thank you very much.

Wisdom & Knowledge Zone

Outer Shway

Fun Shway your Knowledge, Wisdom, and Inner Knowing area when you want to:

* Fine tune your memory and study habits

* Improve your focus and concentration

* Tune into your wise inner self

* Strengthen your intuition

* Activate your psychic powers

* Become a master at anything

* Learn a new language or sport

Wisdom/ Knowledge

Color: Blue
Element: None
Enhancers: Books, desk, scholastic awards, honors, degree, pics of people you admire for their wisdom
Body Part: Hand
Number: 7

The Wisdom and Knowledge Zone of your room is the ideal spot for your desk, a meditation zone, and/or a reading nook.

The most successful people in the world have very clean desktops. Can you guess why? Because it's easier to concentrate, get inspired, and generate new ideas when there isn't a pile of papers competing for your attention. When your desk is clean, so is your mind, which allows for inspiration and creativity. Keep your workspace clean and clutter-free and it will be easier for you to focus on your studies.

Fun Shway Knowledge, Wisdom, & Inner Knowing Activators:

* Items in any shade of blue.

* Books, music, and movies that inspire you or relate to what you want to get better at.

* Diplomas, certificates.

* Decal word art that connects with the quality you want to develop (e.g., peace, kindness, compassion, joy, happiness, tranquility, meditation).

* Candles and light symbolize illumination and can shed light on a difficult problem or subject.

* Make a list of your own values and beliefs and place it here.

* Meditate, read, and do your homework in this part of the room.

* Pictures of people you consider wise and accomplished.

Fun Shway Knowledge, Wisdom, & Inner Knowing Blockers:

* Too many books jam-packed leave no room for new ideas to enter. Weed through your books and only keep the ones you are currently reading, will read, or love.

* If your door is here don't keep it shut all the time. Leave it open to symbolically let in wise people and experts that can help you along your path.

* Paper pileups are no good here.

* Broken light bulbs suggest you may not be thinking clearly.

* Drawers that hardly open make it difficult to access your wisdom and knowledge.

SUCCESS STORY

Monique was struggling in many of her classes. She had a hard time making friends and wasn't motivated to do her homework. When I analyzed her room, I saw that the door, which was positioned in her Wisdom and Knowledge Zone, made a straight line toward a walk-in closet. From a Fun Shway perspective, it appeared that the Chi (life force) was getting funneled and trapped in her closet, which was usually open. I told Monique to keep her closet door closed and hang a multifaceted crystal from the ceiling, between the front door and closet, to divert the energy away from the closet and into her room.

I also noticed that her desk—where she did her homework—was facing a wall. When Monique worked there, her back was to the door. Doors in Fun Shway represent the mouth of opportunity. It's possible that by having her back to the door, Monique was missing valuable opportunities to excel both at school and in her relationships. When we moved her desk around so she could see the room, it placed her in the "command" power position (please find a more detailed explanation of why this is significant in chapter 28).

Within a few months, everything improved. She felt motivated to study and her grades reflected the changes. She even connected with a few girls in her class who she previously thought didn't like her.

CHAPTER 23

Helpful People & Travel: Ask. Believe. Receive.

Inner Shway

Giving and receiving are equally important to being a successful and satisfied human being. Sometimes, the first step in feeling supported is having the courage to ask for what you need. Help comes in many different forms. It may come from people that you know, or sometimes it can appear as an act of random kindness from a stranger, or even the perfect saying that you needed to read on a billboard.

At other times, help comes from an invisible source. This source has many names: God, Light, Angels, Universe, Divine, Guidance, etc.; whatever you want to call it, this source works behind the scenes.

HELPFUL PEOPLE

Ask · Believe · Receive

The act of placing requests to the universe is nothing new. People have been doing it for thousands of years in a state of worship and prayer. One way to ask for help is by writing it down. There is tremendous power in putting your heartfelt desires down on paper and placing them in a Wish Box. I will elaborate more in the exercise below. Trusting that your requests are being received by something greater creates faith in your ability to co-create with the universe!

A very important step when asking for help is to get out of your own way and open yourself to all possibilities. You know you're there when everything comes together and things are better than you could have ever imagined. It's those moments when providence gives you exactly what you need, and you can see that you are a single thread in the tapestry of a mysterious universe.

Fun Shway Time: Creating a Wish Box

The way to access help from this source is to remain open, receptive, generous, and grateful. Although you can ask for help anytime and anywhere, the Helpful People Zone of your room is the best place to put your requests to the universe. Tell it what you want and then be open to receive!

Place a silver or gray container—a box, a bowl, a canister, or a shoebox—in this part of your room, usually the right-hand corner closest to the front door of your room. You can paint it silver or cover it with foil. Write your request in the present tense: "I am so grateful for the wonderful job offer that allows me to travel and have fun doing what I love," or "I'm so thrilled with the like-minded community of friends that I am easily attracting." Power it up by making it specific and juicy! Make sure your requests are at least fifty percent believable. Limit your requests to a maximum of five at a time, as this is the magic number for this zone. Write each request on its own piece of paper. Or you can include a list of all things you would like to achieve in the next one, three, or six months or years. Once you have placed your request in the box, let go of trying to figure out how it's going to show up in your life. Trust that it's in good hands. Remember, you have a team of invisible helpers. Once it's been met, give thanks and throw the paper away!

Helpful People and Travel Zone

Outer Shway

Fun Shway the Helpful People & Travel section of your room when:

* You need extra help in any area of your life

* You want to be in the right place at the right time

* Opening yourself up to all of the opportunities in life

* You have an important interview, test, or meeting

* Receiving guidance from spirit guides

Helpful People/ Travel

Color: Gray
Element: None
Enhancers: Symbols of places you want to travel; pictures of helpful people (e.g., Buddha, Ganesh, Lakshmi, Jesus); religious objects (e.g., Star of David, a cross); hands
Body Part: Head
Number: 5

- ✳ Allowing for universal and earthly support

- ✳ You travel or want to travel

- ✳ You need an extra boost or a push in the right direction

- ✳ You want to experience more miracles in your life

Travel is also represented in this zone—both physical travels, like seeing the world, as well as expanding your sensitivity and awareness to cultures that are different from your own. Cross-cultural sensitivity fosters a sense of peace and oneness and reminds us that we are all connected.

Are you itching to travel? Here's a fun way to manifest some travel opportunities: make a collage on a large white foam board of all the places in the world that you would like to visit. Cut out images, words, and sayings from magazines. Find a current picture of yourself and place it in the center. Then organize and glue your images around your photo. At the bottom of the board write the words, "This or something greater for my highest good and the highest good of all concerned." Close your eyes and say, "Joyful travel opportunities find me now," and visualize yourself jet-setting around the world.

Fun Shway Helpful People and Travel Activators:

- ✳ Gray and silver items.

- ✳ Your Wish Box with your requests to the universe goes here.

- ✳ Get a piece of elegant silver paper and jot down the names of individuals who can assist you in achieving a professional or personal goal. Remember to include your own name, as a reminder of your active role in this journey.

* Get a cork board and pin pictures of all the places you want to travel or put a map here.

* Make a list of all the cool things you are going to do on your trip!

* Add art that depicts heavenly helpers like angels, saints, Jesus, Buddha, etc.

* Pin pictures of the special people in your life who are very helpful to you now (e.g., Mom, your sis, your partner, your feng shui coach, mentors).

* Collect business cards of people you may want to call on in the future.

* Envision and describe your ideal career, then hang it up here so you can see it.

Fun Shway Helpful People and Travel Blockers:

* Anything broken blocks assistance.

* Pictures of people who are not helpful.

* Outdated books that are no longer relevant.

* Words or pictures of things that are self-deprecating and aren't supportive.

* Negative messages and images—no matter how funny they are, they can stick and become beliefs and then your reality.

SUCCESS STORY

Bailey was at the juncture between graduating from high school and choosing her next step in life. She had many interests. Among them were music, art, and design. To make space for greater clarity and decisiveness, I suggested she clear out all the clutter in the Helpful People and Travel Zone of her room, as well as her Prosperity Zone. Once the clutter was gone, she introduced a Fun Shway activator to the Travel/Helpful People Zone. She placed a map of the world and asked the universe to show her where her next destination was. Shortly thereafter, she was invited to stay in San Diego with a relative. Once there, she realized her true passion was to go to art school. She applied and started in the fall. Once she got in command of her space, she was able to listen to the signs, better navigate her life, and figure out the right direction. When you harness the power of feng shui, you align your energy with the highest good for you.

Creativity
awaken your inner artist

CHAPTER 24

Creativity: Awaken Your Inner Artist

Inner Shway

Whether it is art, photography, sewing, music, painting, acting, writing, dancing, improvising, doodling, cooking, coloring, or gardening, everyone has an inner artist. If you want your inner artist to grow, you will need to water him or her every day. Pablo Picasso, Georgia O'Keeffe, and Frida Kahlo clocked hundreds of hours practicing and refining their skills. If you want to write a novel or build a crafting empire, there is only one way: start creating today.

Maybe you've decided that you don't have a creative bone in your body. First, this is impossible. Everyone has an innate ability to create. Even if you aren't interested in art or music, your creative side is important to pay attention to. You might be into collecting shells, rocks, or pinecones, and arranging them in your room. Whatever it is, your creativity may hold the key to unleashing your power.

Are you hiding your art? Is there a gift you have that you worry isn't good enough to develop and share? Not everyone's going to like the same piece of music or writing. When you put too much stock into what other people think, it sucks up all your creative energy. Everyone has something unique to share. Do it for yourself first. The audience will follow. Imagine if Leonardo da Vinci kept the *Mona Lisa* locked in his mind because he thought "Who wants to see another painting of a noblewoman?" Had he kept it in his mind, the world would've lost a great masterpiece.

Don't waste your time trying to figure out if you're good enough. Your job is to get curious, explore, and discover what is inside of you. Pick up the paintbrush, snap a picture, dance in your living room, and just create! Be present and spontaneous, and awaken your inner artist. You might be surprised at what you will find.

Fun Shway Time

Are you ready to get out of a creative rut and into a creative flow? Give your inner artist daily doses of inspiration. Take yourself out on what Julia Cameron, author of *The Artist's Way*, calls an "artist date." Visit places that will inspire your inner muse, like gardens, museums, art galleries, movies, poetry readings, festivals, storytelling events, and live music.

If you can't devote an entire day, I know you can find fifteen minutes. Try this: grab your journal and a pen and just write whatever comes to you. Let your hand keep moving, even if it sounds like complete nonsense. Don't censor yourself. Let your mind unload. Write about anything—what you had for breakfast, who you're angry with, who you love, who you wish you didn't love, what you would rather be doing right now than writing, how annoyed you are with me and this exercise. After about fifteen minutes you might find that you're having a good time and you want to continue. Who knows, maybe a poem will emerge, the beginning of a story, or a memory that you had long suppressed. The result doesn't matter; just getting something written will jump-start your creativity.

Use every opportunity to create. Doodle on napkins while waiting for your mom to serve dinner. Pick up interesting leaves and rocks. Take pictures of those things that inspire or feed your curiosity. Improvise, dance in your room, and sing in your car.

Creativity Zone

Outer Shway

Fun Shway the Creativity Section When:

* You want to learn to paint, write, act, dance, or sew

* You need to finish a creative project

* You need inspiration to create

* You're feeling blocked creatively

* You need creative solutions to difficult problems

Creativity

Color: White, Yellow
Element: Metal
Destructive Element: Fire
Enhancers: Art, music, instruments, bells, crafts, paint, funny and whimsical items, books on creativity
Body Part: Mouth
Number: 3

* You're taking up a new hobby

* You need more joy in your life!

Does your room inspire you? Does it reflect your imagination, unique flare, and signature? Where does your inner artist show up in your bedroom? The creativity section of your room is the perfect zone for your inner artist to shine. Make an inspiration wall where you hang your artwork as well as images of those people, books, ideas, music, and sayings that inspire you. This zone should give you a jolt of inspiration just by standing in it.

Fun Shway Creativity Activators:

* White, metal, and round shapes enhance this section.

* Store your art, paintbrushes, or camera here, so they will be easy to find when you need to take them out and create!

* Create a chalkboard wall and write quotes to inspire your creativity.

* If you have a stereo this is where it goes, along with your music collection.

* Put your board games here, but make sure they aren't creating too much clutter or distracting you from unleashing your creative energy.

* Trying out for a play? Put your monologues and script here. Rehearse here in this section. You can access the energy to help you focus.

* Musical instruments, photography, pens, and journals go here. All things that stimulate your creative juices!

Fun Shway Creativity Blockers:

* If it doesn't inspire you, then it doesn't belong here!

* Too many candles can symbolically melt the metal element that corresponds with this zone.

* A red wall isn't good here.

* Clocks that don't work or that are set to the wrong time can keep your creativity stuck and frozen in time.

SUCCESS STORY

I finished writing and partially editing *Fun Shway* in 2015. Then life happened and I got busy. I told myself I would finish it later. But later never came. I didn't make time for it. When I was finally ready to dive back into my writing, I went to a writers' conference where I met with a publisher who told me, "Young people don't read self-help books." I felt discouraged. I put *Fun Shway* aside and didn't open the file on my computer until 2019.

When I superimposed the Ba-Gua map over my home, I noticed that my closet fell into the Creativity Zone, and it was overflowing with clothing I hadn't worn for many years—clothing that I was afraid to get rid of because of an old belief inherited from my mom that throwing things away, especially clothes, was wasteful and impractical, since fashion always comes back. I knew I couldn't do it alone, so I invited my super creative friend Lia, a very talented jewelry designer and minimalist, to hold me accountable to my own philosophy about only keeping those things that are "Lovables" (from chapter 11, "Making Room for Lovables)".

We spent two days rummaging through my closet and I donated fifty percent of my wardrobe to a transitional homeless shelter that dresses, prepares, and places women in jobs. I did the process again about six months later. The extra space in my closet released enough creative energy for me to finish *Fun Shway*, and here it is!

CHAPTER 25

Give It Your Full Intention

Okay, so you've studied the Ba-Gua, and you know all about the nine areas of life. Now you're ready to amplify the positive energy in your room. Your next step is to go out into the world and find nine objects that have meaning for you that represent each of the nine areas of life in the Ba-Gua. Some of these you may have at home already. Give yourself a few days to collect these objects. The objects should have significant meaning for you. They can be purely symbolic or include either a color and/or element that represents what your intention is. Since you are going to put them all in a bag, it might be best not to pick a car or a horse or something that is bigger than you!

Once you're done collecting them, make a list of the items you found and in what section of the room you will place them. Then introduce each object, one by one, to its corresponding section of your room.

GIVE IT
YOUR FULL
intention

Here are some examples:

Family

A cool piece of wood with an interesting pattern made by a wood-worm on it that you found in the forest behind your house.

Helpful people

A business card or piece of art from one of your mentors to put in your Wish Box.

Romance

Two naturally shaped heart rocks you found on the beach.

Three Reinforcements to Amplify Your Intentions

Now you are going to supercharge your nine objects with three secret reinforcements. This secret technique comes from the BTB school of feng shui (Fun Shway's forefather) and is used to amplify all your intentions. You will need to put your body, speech, and mind into this process. You can accomplish this by using the following three steps. Every time you introduce a Fun Shway enhancer to your room, these three actions will help you reinforce its power and purpose:

> 1. Place and Affirm: Place your object where it needs to go and say your intention for the object out loud. Example: "I place this candle in my Fame Zone so my work is recognized" or "I'm placing this plant here in my Family section to symbolize a strong family foundation" or "I'm placing this picture of myself on a trip to New

York in my Helpful People section to symbolize having more opportunities to travel to New York."

2. Visualize your desired outcome. What does it look and feel like? Imagine it in detail. Use all your senses as you project yourself into a future version of you, where your desire has come to fruition.

3. Give thanks to the object. You can also recite a mantra to help reinforce the intention. It's like the secret sauce that amplifies your intention into the universe. My favorite is the Om Mani Padme Hum, which basically implies that all things have a spark of the divine contained within.

CHAPTER 26

Color Your World

Colors have energy. They can move you into action or help you fall asleep. They can help generate a mood, strike an impression, and evoke a reaction. Painting your own room can be a liberating experience. However, before you turn your room into a giant purple grape or fire-engine red remember that in small doses these colors are impactful and make an impression, but too much of a good thing can be overwhelming.

The Fun Shway Ba-Gua has nine colors that correspond with different life experiences, which I go into in more detail in this chapter. When you're ready to introduce a color into your room, think about the feelings you want to experience, then check the colors and their meanings to see which ones feel right for you. You can paint your entire room or a wall or two, or just pick furnishings and accents, like pillows, sheets, and blankets with the color you love.

Color Your World

If you're not ready to commit to a particular color because you're afraid of how it might look, you can always make a trip to the paint store and get a small sample, paint a section of your wall, live with it for a couple of days, and see how you feel. If you can't live with it, then it's probably a bad match. If you can't get enough of it, then you may have just found your perfect shade.

When placed in their corresponding Ba-Gua zone in the room, colors can strengthen that area of your life. For example, if you want to increase family harmony, add a little green; to strengthen friendships, put some pink tones in the relationship area. Are you catching on?

Pay attention to the colors that you're wearing. Is there a particular color that dominates your closet? How does it make you feel? The colors that touch your skin have a powerful impact on your personal Chi. It's especially effective to use color if you're feeling low on energy. Find the color that carries the energy that you most need at any given moment. You can wear a jacket, sweater, scarf, shirt, pants, or skirt in that color and feel your personal Chi rise.

Colors and Their Meanings

I am listing primary colors here, but there are many hues in each color's family that you can choose from.

Red

Colors in the red spectrum can make you feel anything from pissed off to cozy. Red represents the fire element and can be placed in your room to stimulate the Fame/Self-Image and Power Zones.

Red in Your Bedroom

A word of caution—don't paint your entire room red. Although this color can light a fire under your butt, and help you get things done, too much of this color can make you feel wired. If you are feeling you need more fire, choose a color in the red family and paint one wall (preferably the Fame Zone of your room). Red can be warming, uplifting, and stimulating, and move you into action in an area you've been slacking! However, don't put too much in your Prosperity Zone, since red represents fire, and too much of it can burn up your cash.

Red in Your Wardrobe

Red is an eye-catching, stimulating color. Wear it when you want to stand out, be noticed, get a promotion, or feel empowered for an important presentation. Red is an important ally to have. It will give you more confidence and help get your message across. It can give you the burst of energy you need to accomplish your goals.

Blue

Blue can feel as cool as the ocean on a hot summer day or as calming as floating on a paddle board on a placid lake. Blue calls to mind feelings of tranquility and serenity. It is peaceful, secure, and orderly. Blue represents the Wisdom and Knowledge Zone and can be placed in your room to stimulate that area.

Blue in Your Bedroom

Blue is a great color when you feel overwhelmed. It can relax you and is cooling to the nervous system. Just don't go overboard. Blue is the color of water and too much can put out your fire and literally make you feel "blue."

Blue in Your Wardrobe

Blue is a cozy and comfortable color to wear. Think of your favorite pair of well-worn blue jeans. Don't you just want to kick back and relax in them? Blue calms and makes you feel safe. It can also make you feel smart and sassy when you wear it in a suit, like a navy-blue suit.

Black

Have you ever gone through an all-black phase? It's totally normal to go through a black phase, especially when you're trying to figure out who you are, what you like, and where you're heading in life. Black represents the water element and can be placed in your room to stimulate the Career & Life Path Zone.

Black in Your Bedroom

Black has a certain mysterious and alluring aura about it. It's an introverted color. So, it's great to use during times of transition like adolescence, but too much black in your room might make you feel like you're falling through a big black hole. It can suck out all the good vibes. Go for accents, like picture frames, black-and-white photography, etc.

Black in Your Wardrobe

As the saying goes, every girl needs a little black dress in her closet. Black is glam and a must-have item of couture for many different social settings. It can also be very sleek, and help you blend in and keep a low profile. As many women know, black is slimming. However, if you're trying to stand out in a crowd or make a statement, then you might want to try one of the other eight colors mentioned.

Gray

Gray is best when commingling with an accent color. Too much can cast a gloomy feel and emit an all-around indecisive feeling. In Fun Shway, gray represents the Helpful People and Travel Zone and can be placed in your room to strengthen that area.

Gray in Your Bedroom

The cool, steely, sleek industrial shades of gray may look amazing in your bedroom's color palette when combined with blush, fuchsia, pumpkin orange, or other colors to form a contrast and warm up the freeze. As mentioned before, too much gray in the bedroom can cast an aura of indecision. Don't sleep with gray sheets and bedding or uncertainty may become your predominant mode.

Gray in Your Wardrobe

Okay, so gray may be a fashion basic, but as mentioned, from an energy perspective gray is really an indecisive color. Never wear it when needing to make an important decision or when giving a speech.

Yellow and Orange

Yellow screams sunshine and play. It can wake up your day, transform those winter blues, and get your creative juices flowing. Yellows and oranges awaken, inspire, and stimulate the mind. They're a great cure for moodiness. Yellow helps strengthen the nerves and the mind. In Fun Shway, Yellow and Orange represent the earth element and can strengthen the Health & Healing Zone of your room.

Yellows and Orange in Your Bedroom

If you decide to paint your walls yellow, only paint one wall, or choose a muted yellow for the entire room. A yellow that's too bright can create strain for the eyes over an extended period. Choose a soft yellow that will give you a jolt of sunshine, but still allow you to fall asleep at night.

Yellow and Orange in Your Wardrobe

You don't need to be a walking canary to feel the benefit of yellow in your wardrobe; just add a dab of yellow and orange through a scarf, a pair of socks, an undershirt, or a headband—even a flashy yellow ring or bracelet can be a great finishing touch to brighten up an ensemble.

Green

Your greatest growth spurts and your deepest growing pains happen during young adulthood. Green puts you in touch with nature and the organic world. It reminds you that you're a part of something much larger. It fosters growth and development and will help you keep on track with what's truly important. In Fun Shway, green is symbolic of the wood element and can be used to strengthen the Family and Forgiveness Zone of your bedroom.

Green in Your Bedroom

Green is one of my favorite colors for a bedroom. Having green in your bedroom puts you in touch with the rhythms of nature. Green will nurture and rejuvenate and foster an attitude of peace and patience as you grow. Add a bamboo plant, make it a wall color, or remake your bedding with green accents.

Green in Your Wardrobe

Green can help you feel the nurturing and healing qualities of the natural world. If you are spending too much time in your head or on your phone or computer, green will put you back in touch with your heart. Green is a good color to wear when you want to turn a new leaf or when starting a new project.

Purple

Purple is the color for royalty, abundance, prosperity, and the feeling of "I am worthy." Historically, only kings and queens wore purple, because it was a very difficult and expensive dye to obtain. In Fun Shway, purple represents the Prosperity Zone and can be placed in your room to strengthen that area.

Purple in Your Bedroom

Having purple in your bedroom can make you feel very opulent, like you are the empress or emperor of your own castle. It can also strengthen your "crown chakra," an area at the top of your head that is associated with receiving divine inspiration. Leonardo da Vinci believed the power of meditation increases when imagining purple light.

Purple in Your Wardrobe

Just like red, purple can make you stand out, but in a much more refined and polished way. Whenever I feel worried about money, I throw on a shade of purple and become queen for the day! Purple nail polish works great too.

White

White conveys purity, clarity, and focus; also creativity. The white canvas calls to us. It craves to be painted, colored, and collaged. In Fun Shway, white is symbolic of the metal element and represents the Creativity Zone of your room, and can be used to strengthen this area.

White in Your Bedroom

There is something pristine about having stark white walls. They inspire creativity and make you feel like anything is possible! White stirs up your imagination and supports clear thinking, but too much in your room creates a feeling of sterility and rigidity. Try adding a white dry-erase board or an easel with canvas to your room. It will beckon the flow of creativity.

White in Your Wardrobe

Wear white when you want to generate fresh ideas or when you are starting a creative project. Any special occasion like New Year's Eve is the ideal time to wear white. White can help you keep your mind open and deflects negativity. I love wearing white when I teach because it reminds me to stay open and welcome inspiration.

Pink

Think of Valentine's Day and the hundreds of little pink candy hearts that fill your pockets and mouth. Think of pink flamingos, pink roses, pink bubble gum, and cotton candy. Pink is associated with love and all the expressions of giving and receiving love. In Fun Shway, pink represents the Relationship Zone and can be used in your room to strengthen that area.

Pink in Your Bedroom

Having pink in your bedroom can be a fun and girly choice, adding a touch of femininity and romance to your space. But be cautious – too much pink could lead to an overdose of feminine energy, which might leave you feeling passive, like a wallflower in a quiet corner. Consider blush, a more muted shade of pink, to bring sophistication, while splashes of hot pink or fuchsia call for attention.

Pink in Your Wardrobe

Pink is soft, gentle, romantic, and loving, and it is a perfect color for a first date, a spring day, or a special event like a wedding. Pink is also very approachable and conveys an open heart. Wear it when you would like to make new friends or have a heart-to-heart talk. I like wearing pink in a scarf or accessory like a headband. Pink is great in a dainty flowing dress, a jazzy leather jacket, or an artsy scarf.

YIN & YANG: YOU CAN'T HAVE ONE WITHOUT THE OTHER

CHAPTER 27

Yin and Yang: You Can't Have One Without the Other

Everything in life has its opposite. What comes up must come down. Nothing stays the same. Broken hearts mend and the winter blues eventually go away. And no matter where you live, the sun is bound to shine sooner or later.

When you learn how to balance these energies you can stop living like a yo-yo and start living like a yogi. All the differences in our universe are just opposite sides of the same coin. The coin is the Tao: the universal principle of oneness that underlies everything.

Have you ever seen the symbol at the start of this chapter? Even if you haven't, I'm sure you have felt its presence in your life. These two forces are called Yin and Yang. They represent the opposites in life: sad/happy, dark/light, warm/cold, short/tall, tight/loose, soft/hard, plump/svelte, introvert/extrovert, and female/male.

Each of these forces exists in relation to the other. You can't truly understand the effects of one without first having experienced the other. Don't let the black-and-white thing fool you, though. It's not as simple as good and bad or right and wrong. These two forces are complementary—and not that judgmental! When used collaboratively, Yin and Yang can help you to create a harmonious life.

Fun Shway Time: Yin & Yang Tune-Up

Peek into your bedroom and ask yourself some of these questions:

* Do I have too many frilly, pink things?

* Am I holding onto childhood toys and dolls?

* Is it hard to walk through my room without tripping on clutter?

* Do I feel kind of sluggish and unmotivated most of the time?

* Do I find it hard to go to the gym or socialize and make new friends?

* Would I rather stay in my room at night and read than go out with friends?

If you answered yes to most of these, then your bedroom may be suffering from a Yin overdose. Here are a few more questions that will help you determine this:

* Am I eating mostly junk food?

* Do I talk for hours on my phone and send a gazillion texts (even during work time?)

* Do I have so many posters and prints that they are starting to look like wallpaper?

* Is my email inbox overflowing?

If this feels like your life, then you are living in an extreme Yang lifestyle. To live in harmony, you need the Yin and Yang in your life in moderation!

Where Are You on the Scale?

Put on your Fun Shway goggles and look at your room and your life from a Yin and Yang perspective. The chart below is a list of characteristics of a Yin and Yang lifestyle. Place a checkmark near the word that feels like the best fit for you and your room. Once you are done, add them up and write the number in the empty columns below. The column that has the most checkmarks is your predominant inclination on the Yin/Yang scale.

The Yin life and her attributes	The Yang life and his attributes
Black, blue, dark green	Red, hot orange, bright yellow
Soft	Hard
Dark	Bright
Low	High

Ocean	Desert
Moon	Sun
Quiet	Loud
Clutter	Organization
Curvy	Straight
Round	Square
Slow	Fast
Embroidered/ flowy	Geometric
Suburbs	City
Meditate	Socialize
Sleep	Work out
Chill	Create
Contracting	Expanding
Cool	Warm

Quiet	Loud
Introverted	Extroverted
Passive/follower	Active/leader
Study	Party
Feeling	Thinking
Intuition	Sense
Spiritual	Physical
Total:	**Total:**

Heavy on the Yang

If your scale is tipping heavily on the Yang side, you might need to offset some of that quaking energy. You know you are tipping the scale with too much Yang if your lifestyle feels way out of control. But no worries, it's easy to balance out. Spend time alone in nature and reflect on the beauty that surrounds you. Reading, meditation, and restorative yoga can all produce a more Yin lifestyle.

If your life feels like there is always drama on the rise, even if it's not your drama, then that's a surefire sign that you are in a Yang environment. Creating a drama-free Yin zone can be simple. Find a place you can chill where you won't be bothered. If you can't achieve this in your room, there is also the great outdoors.

Simply walking on the grass barefoot, hugging a tree, or walking on the beach can balance and ground your Yang energy and help you feel more serene.

Heavy on the Yin

If your scale is tipping heavily on the Yin energy side, it won't hurt to put the books down for a night and go out with friends to a movie. The juicy novel you are reading will still be there when you get home.

Sluggish, low energy is just as contagious as the common cold, so if you find yourself surrounded by people who are always down, depressed, bored, complaining, and would rather stay at home most of the time, then you might want to join a club or start a hobby. If you really like being home a lot, then have a sleepover and invite your friends occasionally.

Anything in extreme will usually backfire later. The universe has a way of helping you to self-correct. For example, if you're not taking time for self-care, you may get a cold, which will force you to spend more time at home. If you're frequently going out, noticing missed appointments and unchecked items on your to-do list could signal that life is becoming a bit unmanageable. Balance is key to experiencing Yin/Yang harmony.

Fun Shway Time

1. Is your bedroom predominantly more Yin or Yang?

2. If you see that you are tipping the scale, can you add some attributes from the opposite side of the column to your room and/or life? Which ones can you implement today?

3. How do the principles of Yin and Yang play out in your life? Use both your bedroom and your lifestyle to answer this question.

4. What can you do to create more balance in your room and in your life?

Get into Command

Use your Bed and Desk to Take Command of Your Life

CHAPTER 28

Get Into Command: Use Your Bed and Desk to Take Command of Your Life

It's kind of crazy to think about, but you spend one-third of your time, or thirty percent of your life, in bed. That means your bed and its placement can either be a source of rest and rejuvenation, or it could be depleting your good Chi. The location of your bed can help you feel either more replenished and secure, or vulnerable and anxious.

In Fun Shway, we have an optimal spatial arrangement for your bed. It's called the **Command Position.** As mentioned, the command position is the ideal placement to support feelings of safety and a good night's sleep. The same rule applies to your desk. Placing your desk in the command position encourages focus and concentration.

Below you will find an illustration with both favorable (Command Position) and unfavorable locations for your bed. If the current position of your bed is in the left column (unfavorable), please move it to one of the three favorable placements on the right.

The Command Position for Your Bed

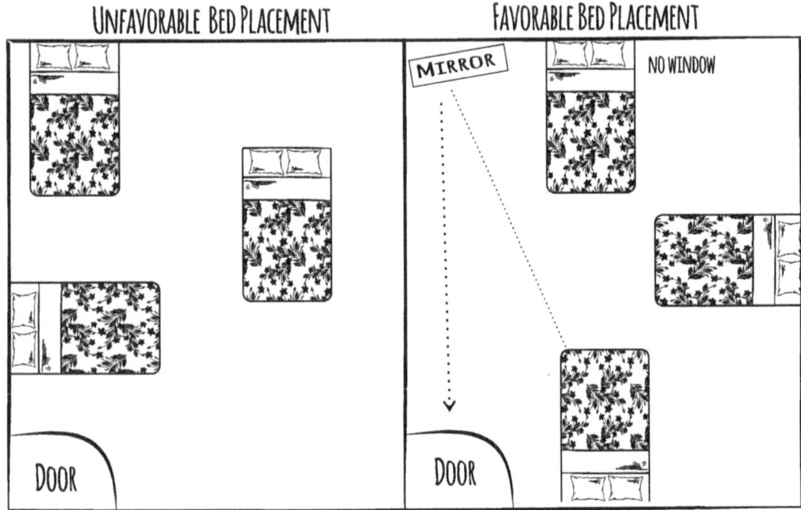

* From where you are sleeping, you should have the widest view of the room and see the door (but not sleep directly in front of it). This is the optimal position for feeling empowered and safe.

* Ideally, your headboard should be placed against a solid wall for maximum security and support.

* Create enough space around the bed so Chi can circulate freely.

* When you can't see the door from where you are sleeping, your flight or fight response system gets triggered. This setup can dysregulate your nervous system and leave you feeling anxious and on edge.

* Sleeping directly in front of the door is called the Line of Fire, and the energy flows too quickly. Over time, the fast-moving Chi can contribute to a stress response in the body.

* Stay clear of placing the bed or desk under a window. Fun Shway considers this an insecure placement where personal Chi can fly out and leave you feeling depleted. If there is no way around it, then make sure to hang a multifaceted crystal between your head and window for protection. The crystal will contain your good Chi and keep it from leaving.

* Don't let your bed float more than a foot from the wall (as seen in the illustration on page 202—left column.) Otherwise, you might feel like your life is unmoored, floating away, en route to some uncertain place. Over time, this arrangement can cause feelings of aimlessness.

* When your bed is situated along the same wall as the door to your room, as seen at the bottom of the box in the right column, "Favorable Bed Placement," it creates a blind spot, which can be remedied by placing a mirror kitty-corner so you can easily see the door from where you are sleeping. It's called the Virtual Command Position and will be explored further on page 205.

The Command Position for Your Desk

Notice that in this illustration even unfavorable placements have their most and least constructive. For example, although still unfavorable, #1 is better than #2 and #3. The same goes for favorable placements where #1 is better than #2, which is better than #3, and so on.

* Make sure to sit in a chair with a straight and solid back (no gaps). Your back must be up against a solid wall (ideally there shouldn't be a window behind you). If there is and you can't move your desk, hang a crystal between your desk and window to keep your Chi from flying out.

* An unobstructed view of the door from where you are sitting is essential.

* If your desk directly faces a wall, it can lead to feeling blocked. Either move your desk so you have the widest view of the room or position a mirror in front of you so you can see what's behind you. You can also hang a picture with an image that creates the illusion of depth and expansion, like a road, the mountains, or the ocean.

Take the Virtual Command Position

As mentioned earlier, when you can't see the door from where you sleep or study you may be missing important opportunities. But there is a way to remedy this dilemma.

It's called the **Virtual Command Position.** By placing a mirror that reflects the door from where you are working and sleeping, you place yourself in the command position. The mirror creates a rearview perspective like the rearview mirror in a car. It has your back and protects you from being startled.

If you have a desktop computer, you can purchase a desktop mirror at **www.monitormirror.com.** However, any mirror that allows you to see what's behind you works just as well.

Use Your Doors to Create Opportunity

Doors are the mouth of Chi. They can either open gracefully or not. If they are sticky, then the Chi gets stuck. All the doors should open with ease. That means no clutter behind the door. If you want opportunities to enter, then your doors must open to their full potential.

CHAPTER 29

Your Room's Elemental Balance

Water, earth, metal, fire, and wood are the building blocks of our physical world. Out of all the planets in our solar system, Earth has life because of the presence and balance of these five elements. If one of these elements were missing it might throw off the entire ecosystem and life as we know it could cease to exist.

Can you imagine living without water or the warmth of the sun? According to Fun Shway, we need to balance these five elements in our homes to thrive. Our well-being depends on it! If you look around, you will see all five elements represented in our physical world.

In Fun Shway, the ideal place to live is where we can experience all four seasons. Ultimately, life takes us where we need to go. But when the choice is yours, try and pick a climate that suits your temperament, or where the dominant season helps you thrive.

Your Room's Elemental Balance

In my hometown of Seattle, the presence of all four seasons creates a natural balance and provides lush trees and forests. I grew up surrounded by mountains and lakes and the ocean, all of which have amazing energy. But Seattle gets 260 overcast days a year, which contributes to a high rate of seasonal affective disorder (SAD), a depression-related condition that stems from long periods of darkness and not enough exposure to sunlight.

I'm deeply sensitive to the weather and felt gloomy most of the time. As a young adult who suffered from bouts of SAD, I noticed a significant lift in my mood when I moved from Seattle to Los Angeles, and then later to Miami Beach. Although I missed the lush forests and the lakes, I could also see that getting more sunlight was really healing for me.

In Fun Shway, the fire element is represented by the sun, which provides us with vitamin D and helps our brains produce serotonin, a neurotransmitter, which regulates mood, sleep, and digestion. The sun is responsible for many important things. It helps us get out of bed in the morning and function in the world. Many people who live in regions that don't get enough sun have to find alternative ways of raising their serotonin levels, like getting more exercise or using a lamp that simulates sunlight.

If you happen to live in a place with little nourishment from the warm rays of the sun, you can compensate with more exercise to release dopamine and vitamin D3 to encourage serotonin production. Another thing you can do is to dress up your room with happy, bright images and natural lighting, and surround yourself with bright, nurturing, uplifting people. This alignment with the fire element in Fun Shway symbolizes warmth, transformation, and dynamic energy in our lives.

Balance in Your Environment

Ready to create the balance you need to thrive? The first thing you'll need to do is take an elemental reading of your room, which can be found on page 212.

In Fun Shway, all indoor accessories and furniture can be reduced to their respective elements. You can learn how to bring the color and the shape associated with each element and use it as an enhancement or cure. Here are some examples of items that relate to the elements that will help harmonize your space.

Fire

* Red

* Candles, incense, matches, a fireplace

* Pictures with the fire element

* Pyramids and stars (come to a point and symbolize a flame)

* Hair dryer, fur, electric items placed up high, leather, pointy objects

Wood

* Green

* Any type of wood: wicker, bamboo, oak, acacia, redwood, cedar, etc.

* Plants or trees

* Straw and cotton

* Rectangular and columnar objects because they symbolize a tree trunk

* Pictures of trees and forests (use wood picture frames)

* Tables, chairs

* Flooring and mats made from wood

Metal

* White

* All metal (this includes electronics)

* Glass and mirrors

* Chimes

* Circular objects

* Gold and silver jewelry and coins

Earth

* Brown, orange, or yellow

* Ceramics

* Terra cotta, rocks, and sand

* Shells, coral

* Square objects

Water

* Black
* Water fountain
* Pictures of water
* Mirrors (they symbolize the water element in Fun Shway)
* Vases or cups with water
* Undulating shapes, representing the waves in the ocean
* Fish tanks

Fun Shway Time: Elemental Reading

Walk through your room and make a list of how many elements below appear in your space. Then add up the number of elements for each. Are most of the things in your room wood and fire? Are water and metal missing? Take notes.

Wood	Metal	Fire	Water	Earth

Total:	**Total:**	**Total:**	**Total:**	**Total:**

Too Much of a Good Thing

Too much of one element in your room may create an imbalance, even an overdose of something in your life. A typical element that I've found out of balance in many people's homes is wood. Wood floors, wood bed, wood dresser, drawers, wood paneling (okay, mostly in the 1970s). Some people have wood *everything*. What does any of this have to do with how you feel or think? Well, a lot actually! What are some qualities that come to mind when you think of wood? What comes to mind for me is:

Strong

Firm

Steady

Secure

These are all great qualities. But when those qualities are out of balance, it can lead to too much stubbornness and not enough flow. Too much firmness, and not enough bounce or levity in your life. A room in which everything is made of wood can start to feel very heavy. Sometimes too much wood is an indicator of needing to be in control of everything and of being very headstrong and inflexible.

An excess of these elements can lead to:

Wood	Stubbornness and resistance.
Metal	Curt and hurtful language. Uncomfortable. Unfriendly. Destructive. Scattered attention and lack of focus.
Fire	Temperamental. Jumpy. Impulsive. Burnout. Hysteria. Mania.
Water	Emotional upset and upheaval. Sadness. Self-pitying. Constant complaining. Depression.
Earth	Stuck. Rigid. Hard to get projects off the ground. Fear of letting go.

A balance of these elements promotes:

Wood	Strong, firm, steady, secure, account-able, upward movement.
Metal	Creative, sturdy, focus, sharp mind. The ability to cut through nonsense.
Water	Flexible, flowing, receptive, nourish-ing, calming, tranquil, artistic; fosters communication.
Fire	Warming, energizing, action-orient-ed, vibrant, attention-getting, outgo-ing, expressive.
Earth	Stable, practical, down-to-earth, grounded.

When your room is lacking one or more of these elements, it can manifest as a negative or lacking effect in some area of your life. For example, when there's not enough:

Wood: No backbone or courage; too challenging to commit or stand up for yourself

Water: Inflexible; can't communicate your ideas; confused or muddy thinking

Earth: Ungrounded

Metal: Dull and slow; too quiet, cautious, or careful

Fire: Challenging to get projects going, not enough steam

Once you've done an elemental reading of your room, you will next want to make sure that the elements are represented in their corresponding zones of the Ba-Gua. Use the Ba-Gua grid for the ideal placement of each element.

Family: Wood

Health and Healing: Earth

Creativity: Metal

Career: Water

Self-Image/Respect: Fire

Maybe you have too much metal in the Family Zone and it's chopping up the wood, or all the water in your Fame Zone is putting out your fire. As you strive for elemental balance, you can make little changes along the way. Let's say your bed is metal and it's in the wood section (Family Zone) of your bedroom, and it doesn't make sense to move it anywhere else in the room. Don't stress out. You've got Fun Shway to show you the way. In this case, the element that would destroy the metal is fire, also represented by the color red. So, you add some red pillows, sheets, or blankets. Or hang a painting with a little red in it, or a photograph that depicts fire, the sun, or any object in the fire element. A little red goes a long way and can strike the right balance. Fun Shway is about creating an environment that makes you feel good.

	FIRE	
WOOD	EARTH	METAL
	WATER	

front door *front door* *front door*

Fun Shway Time

Want to welcome the power of nature into your space? Go out and find examples of all five elements in nature and bring the ones you need more of into your room. Notice how you feel as the energy changes immediately. Write your observations here.

CHAPTER 30

Quick Reference for Better Chi, Abundant Energy, and a Spectacular Room

By now you have learned a whole lot about Fun Shway. You also understand that Chi is the ever-present swirling life force energy that, if invited in and used wisely, can transform your room—and your life. The more Chi you collect, the better you feel and the more aligned you will be with the universe. With good Chi around you, all things flow to you and life becomes a river of abundance.

You deserve a spectacular clutter-free mind and a room that inspires you to be your best self. Here's some quick Fun Shway tips I've already covered as well as a few more simple but powerful one's to harness the Chi and the life force energy that will bring harmony and balance to your space and your life:

* Make sure you can see the front door from where you are sleeping and working.

* To feel in command of your room and life, maintain the widest view of the room from where you place your bed, a.k.a. the Command Position.

* Let go of things that aren't serving you any longer, including stuff from the past that makes you sad.

* Introduce fresh flowers or plants to raise the life force energy in your room.

* Fix broken items or let them go.

* Mirrors in front of your bed bounce light and can make it difficult to wind down and fall asleep. If you have a large closet door mirror, cover it with a curtain.

* Introduce pops of orange and red to increase vitality, but don't have unnecessary red in your room unless you want to stay up all night.

* Leave open spaces for new ideas and inspiration to enter.

* Heavy items hanging over your bed make life feel oppressive.

* When you sleep under a beam or a low-slanted ceiling, your life force energy will feel compromised. Camouflage beams with fabric, prayer flags, tapestries, lights, etc.

* Too many images of water will make you feel like you're drowning.

* A plethora of stuff under your bed stagnates energy.

* Declutter books you aren't currently reading on your nightstands, or you'll have a hard time shutting down your brain.

* Introduce all five elements—wood, earth, fire, water, and metal—to create a comfort zone.

* Make sure your Yin/Yang is balanced!

* Watch out for anything that could compromise feelings of security (e.g., having a window behind your head, not being able to see the door, sharp corners pointing at you).

* If there is a window directly behind your bed, your Chi may be flying away while you sleep. To remedy this, hang a multifaceted crystal ball between you and the window.

* Use the Ba-Gua to pick colors that correspond with the qualities you want to experience and express more of in your life.

* Holding on to gifts or reminders from your ex will keep them hanging on to you.

* Don't have your back facing the door when sleeping or working, or you could feel more vulnerable and less in command of your life.

* If you absolutely can't move your desk or bed to be in the command position, place a mirror so you can see what's behind you.

* Objects placed or hung high on the wall will help set your sights high and remind you of your highest aspirations.

* Stones, drums, or rugs on the ground will support you to feel rooted.

* Having adequate space around your belongings will help you collect positive Chi.

* To attract a relationship or more friends into your life, place objects and pictures of pairs in the right-hand corner of the room opposite the front door.

* Make sure the doors to your room open smoothly without any screeching, whining sounds. Annoying or nagging sounds can invite unpleasant people and situations.

* Don't keep your bed tousled and unkempt because it will deplete your life force and make you feel like you're never ready.

* If you can see your bed from where you are studying, it can make you tired. Use a divider or a plant to create an illusion of separate spaces.

* Keep the TV out of your bedroom or cover it up.

* State your affirmations out loud every day and declare your desires to the universe.

The End is Just the Beginning

When I told my dad that I was going to be a feng shui consultant he said, "Fuk shvay, what kind of sushi is that?" It took my family years to wrap their minds—and their tongues—around my chosen profession. They were so confused about my career plans that for the first couple of years they told all their friends and our extended family that I was an interior designer because they found it easier to explain. They wanted to believe that this "fuk shvay" business was just a phase. Fortunately, I never backed down from my dreams of Shwaying the world one room at a time and twenty years later, *Fun Shway: A Feng Shui Guide for Young Adults—Change Your Room, Change Your Life* is finally ready to be born.

Although they aren't yet firm believers, these days my parents will consult with me for Fun Shway cures and blessings when looking to buy a property. I believe Fun Shway had a lot to do with the transformation of my family into a unit of support and encouragement. But the change couldn't happen until I started to Fun Shway myself first. Mindfully rearranging my room helped me straighten out my thoughts, heal my wounds, and forgive myself and others. It also helped to manifest some of my heartfelt desires.

My hope is that you will find at least one gem in this book, one that resonates with you and brings more joy, peace, and harmony into your life—wherever you are on your path and wherever you choose to live.

Remember though, your true home is always inside of you. It lives in your heart.

I hope that Fun Shway has given you some new tools to have at your disposal to create whatever you want or need at this moment in your life. The smallest steps can render the biggest results if you make them consistently and diligently. Now you know that if you ever feel stuck you can move something a few inches to the right or left, add a little of this, get rid of some of that. And most importantly of all, keep the energy in your room or your space moving. Even though this is the end of our time together, it's just the beginning of your adventure with Fun Shway!

APPENDIX

Case Studies

I hope you found the ideas and principles in this book inspiring. For those who want to go deeper into the process, I've included two case studies below from my psychology graduate school thesis where I explored Fun Shway as a psychological tool for discovering one's unique identity and laying the foundation for success in life.

We went through the same steps mentioned in the previous chapters and here's what happened.

Meet Amy and Alex

Amy was sixteen when we met—a year from graduating from high school and leaving her parents' home to attend college. She shared that "senior year started out incredibly stressful" and that she felt "helpless and stuck." She was confused about what career path to take and which college to attend. She was feeling very unsettled and wanted more clarity about her direction. It was time to redefine herself as she moved into the next phase of her life.

AMY'S ROOM SHWAY

Looking around the room, it was obvious that her bedroom had become a dumping ground for clutter and things that were no longer relevant or useful to her. Amy was aware that her room was "a mess." She explained that she had changed rooms a few years back, but never felt like she fully "moved in."

Amy didn't invest much energy into her new room. Her unique interests and personality were absent from her space. The same lack of intention and uncertainty was showing up in her life.

As I analyzed her space, I pointed to a strange marking of a half-finished stencil of a star located on the wall behind the bed with what appeared to be blotchy handprints. According to Amy, this was a project she started but never finished, and wasn't the least bit interested in completing. I pointed to the areas that were taken over by clutter and asked what in the room, if anything, Amy truly loved. Based on her frown, I could tell that there was nothing. She told me that she just wanted to start over.

Phase I

First, I drew upon the space-clearing recipe from chapter 12, *Clear the Way for Awesome Shway*. Once the old energy was cleared, Amy felt much lighter and was ready to start decluttering her room. She said, "I felt a sense of relief right away."

Phase II

Next, I had Amy draw her room's floor plan from an aerial (bird's eye) perspective. We overlaid the Ba-Gua template (see chapter 14), so she could see what parts of her room corresponded with the nine areas of life on the Ba-Gua map. We explored the cluttered areas in her room and their relationship to the zones on the Ba-Gua. There's often a connection between a person's clutter, where it exists on the Ba-Gua map (i.e., the corresponding zone), and where there might be a block. I will go into greater detail below.

We jumped to the next step, which was to start the clutter-clearing process right away. Amy used my four-step method of identifying clutter by asking the questions:

1. Do I really USE it?

2. Do I LOVE it?

3. Does it belong here?

Then she separated the items into five boxes:

1. GIVE AWAY

2. THROW AWAY

3. SELL (on eBay, Craigslist, garage sale, or Amazon)

4. TRANSITION (for items that may belong someplace other than your room or in a different location in your room)

5. COME BACK IN SIX MONTHS (for items that you need to step away from and reconsider)

Decluttering opened space and brought clarity. Amy shared: "It really helped me clear out the useless items I had, but also to realize what was important enough to keep in my life." Through clearing the clutter and only keeping those things that she considered Lovable, and introducing symbols that held meaning for her, the room began to reflect more accurately Amy's true self, and this infused her with confidence and life force.

Before Fun Shway

Prosperity Zone: There were about thirty different empty bags from various department stores crammed away behind the dresser, and dozens of beauty products competed for space. Amy is no bag lady, and these bags were choking her abundance and good Chi.

Self-Image/Power Zone: This section contained one of three sloping ceilings. Slopes create an oppressive energy in the room. There was also a hidden bulletin board blocked by pillows, some laminated exercise charts she never looked at, and random things that had little meaning for her. The combination of slopes and things that held no meaning for Amy were oppressing her personal power. This area was lacking in attention and needed to be infused with some love and intention. Amy put all these items on eBay. Cha-ching!

Helpful People/Travel Zone: The bed was positioned in a vulnerable spot with her back to the door. A door in Feng shui represents the mouth of opportunity. Amy's door was out of sight, which was disempowering and blocked her ability to see her opportunities and choices. The wall above and behind her bed is also where a half-finished stencil of a star lived.

Career/Life Purpose Zone: An oversized desk stood near the bed and was acting as a clutter collector.

After Fun Shway

The following are the Fun Shway fixes that Amy implemented based on my suggestions and her creative inspiration.

All nine zones: The room was painted a refreshing mint green (Amy's chosen color).

Prosperity Zone: All the bags behind the dresser were tossed! A lovely little arrangement of family photos and sentimental items on a small table that represented what was truly valuable to Amy replaced the bulky dresser.

Self-Image/Power Zone: The oppressive slants were covered with Amy's choice of tapestries and fabric to soften and create a more intimate and cozier feel to the room.

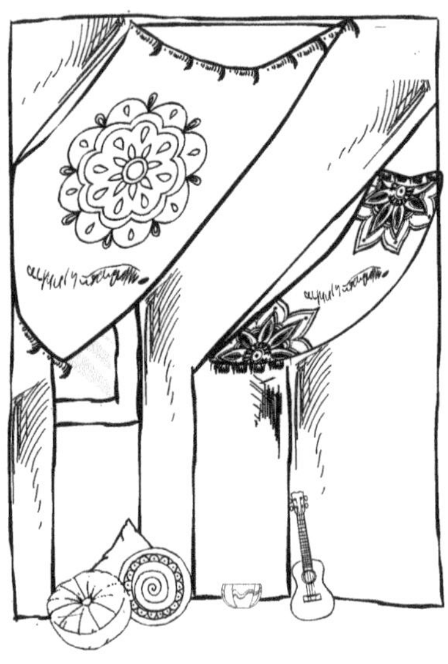

Helpful People/Travel Zone: The bed was moved into the Command Position so she could have the widest view of the room, see the door, and be on the receiving end of opportunities. Since this is the Helpful People Zone, Amy chose a picture of Buddha's eyes to hang over the bed to help reinforce serenity and mindfulness while making decisions regarding what college she would attend.

Career/Life Purpose Zone: Amy tossed the clutter, and a smaller, more functional desk replaced the large overpowering desk.

Amy wrote her ideal scene for the college she wanted to attend and placed it in a box near her bed. A beautiful wall tapestry of a lion, representing courage and power, was hung behind her bed in order to draw on those energies when making life decisions.

My Fun Shway Assessment

Amy had never fully moved into her bedroom. Similarly, she was tentative about starting the next chapter of her life. Her room was hanging in a state of limbo. She was caught in between adolescence and adulthood. Amy was now ready to create a space that truly reflected her transition from life at home to a new beginning in college.

Amy's energy was being drained by the belongings that cluttered her room—things she did not care for nor make much use of. It was my intention to help her come home to herself.

Deciding on the next step was of the utmost importance to Amy. Consciously arranging her room to reflect her interests and what was most valuable to her was an essential ingredient in cultivating more self-esteem. Fun Shway helped Amy release the clutter and identify what was important and meaningful to her, and placed Amy on the right path. Clearing her clutter helped clear her mind of all the competing wishes, intentions, and pressure she was placing on herself.

Moving her bed to the "command position" (as discussed in chapter 28) placed Amy in command of her room, which resulted in her making empowered choices. Covering the oppressive architecture with tapestries created a serene feel and offset the heaviness she was experiencing in her room and life.

Moreover, buying a smaller desk made it possible for Amy to have more space in her room. She also became more inclined to use the desk, whereas before, it was just another clutter collector. Because the desk was in the Life Path/Career Zone in her room, making the desk fit was symbolic of finding the right fit for college. With these few small steps, she was now on the right track.

Applying the principles of Fun Shway allowed Amy to harness her energy and direct it toward creating a space that revealed her unique personality, which gave her the confidence to decide her next step in life. She applied and got into one of the top three colleges on her wish list.

In Amy's words:

> At first, I didn't know if I believed Fun Shway would work, but it already has! I have completed my first goal; I have decided where I want to go to college. I know this is the place I am meant to be, and I would have never been able to come to this conclusion without the help of Inessa and my new space. I can think more clearly and be at peace in my room now. My future is surely uncertain, but with my ideal scenes and my serene personal space, I know I will now be able to achieve whatever goals I put in front of me.

ALEX'S ROOM SHWAY

Alex, a nineteen-year-old college freshman, aspiring musician, and singer, was ready for a big change. Alex's room was frozen in time. It hadn't changed since she was fourteen. Alex told me that fourteen was the last time she felt truly happy.

At the time of our meeting, I discovered that her parents were going through a divorce, and she'd just broken up with her boyfriend. As if breaking up wasn't hard enough, Alex's ex-boyfriend left her with a swarm of bed bugs.

Alex lamented, "Bed bugs are horrible and the trauma of getting about forty new bites a day has somewhat scarred me internally. I get really nervous being in my room because I don't know if they are completely dead or not." According to Alex, shortly after she had discovered the bed bugs in her room, things in life started to "bug" her in a "big way." Alex said she was feeling depressed about her life and was ready to stop feeling like a kid.

Alex said, "I haven't really been sure what my real home is for the last eight months. And I don't really like calling my parents' house home. It's not really my parents' house anymore because of the divorce. My dad is still living here, and my parents are good roommates. It's just not a suitable environment for me to be in right now, but I don't really have a choice."

Every person is different, as is every Fun Shway experience. The makeover for Alex's bedroom is described in more depth than the previous makeover due to the dynamic nature of her life situation.

During our first session, Alex seemed down. She had bags under her eyes and looked like she had not slept much the night before. One thing was loud and clear: she was ready for change.

Alex's room was very cluttered. It was like walking into a much younger person's room. Stuffed animals and toys found their way to every empty countertop, and a few jumbo-sized ones were suspended from the ceiling.

I asked Alex, "If your room had a voice, what would it say about you?" Her response was:

My room is very fun, but it's not tied together by anything. It's just kind of scattered. I haven't changed my room since I was fourteen. If my room had a voice it would say, "Help Me!" It represents a very immature version of who I used to be. I used it a lot to prove that I wasn't boring when I was younger because I didn't have a lot of friends in middle school and high school. I kind of used it to look cool when people would come over.

Alex was ready to redefine herself. "Redoing my room will help me figure out my taste and help me figure out more of who I am." Although Alex carried a lot of attachment to her belongings, her strong desire to mature and come into her own was apparent. "I want to stop being a kid, and this room doesn't help me do that."

Together, we established that Alex's primary goal was to help her reclaim her room so that it would reflect the person she was now. Alex's secondary goal was to make more friends. She was having a hard time keeping friends and felt like she spent a lot of time "pushing people away." Moreover, Alex's long-term goal was to own her own record label. The most important and immediate need, however, was to reduce the amount of clutter and bring some order to her space.

Just like the previous makeover for Amy, I suggested that Alex use my four-step method of identifying clutter by asking these questions:

1. Do I really USE it?

2. Do I LOVE it?

3. Does it belong here?

I suggested that even before she partook in the clutter-clearing process, she should engage in a sacred ritual of letting go. I encouraged her to go through each possession to which she still felt attached from when she was younger, touch it, and thank it for being a part of her life and serving her up until now.

This process honors the symbolic meaning of each item in service of letting go of things that no longer support you by acknowledging that those things were valuable at one point but have fulfilled their purpose, and now it's time to move on. I suggested that once Alex completed clearing her clutter, she would only introduce items to her room that she loved. Next, I performed the Space Clearing ritual for her room, to clear the energy imprints on her belongings and to loosen her attachment to them.

When we discussed Alex's vision for her room, she shared that she wanted a black, red, and white color scheme. Red seemed appropriate because in feng shui it is considered a power color. To replace her bright pink bedding, she wanted a black comforter that had an image of a glow-in-the-dark monster, with wording that said, "Come to the dark side, we have cookies."

I explained to Alex that in feng shui, when young adults pick the color black as a dominant color for either the walls or bedding, it usually represents their quest to figure out who they are. According to feng shui and space-clearing expert Karen Kingston (1997) in her book, Creating Sacred Space With Feng Shui, "Black symbolizes the void of transition, and many teenagers go through a 'black phase' when they are finding themselves" (p. 3). In addition, black absorbs light and does not reflect anything; it is an introverted color. Alex's clever response was, "Yeah, and it's not even a color."

I brought Alex's attention to the fact that the monster on her new choice of bedding also looked like a bed bug and that she would literally be sleeping with one every night. Moreover, I decided to push the point a little further and asked, "Do you want to put yourself back into bed with another bed bug?"

I wanted to honor Alex in her process, and I understood that choosing black over her bright pink bedding may have been her way of making a statement; yet my intuitive sense was that the dark color and the image might depress her energy even more as well as perpetuate the unhealthy relationship.

I encouraged Alex to use symbolic eyes and spend some more time researching to find an alternative to the bedding set she picked—one that perhaps would create the ambience she wanted to experience. My feedback seemed to ring true for her, and she was eager to look for new bedding. Alex ended up choosing ivory-colored sheets to bring in a clean and fresh neutral feel to her space.

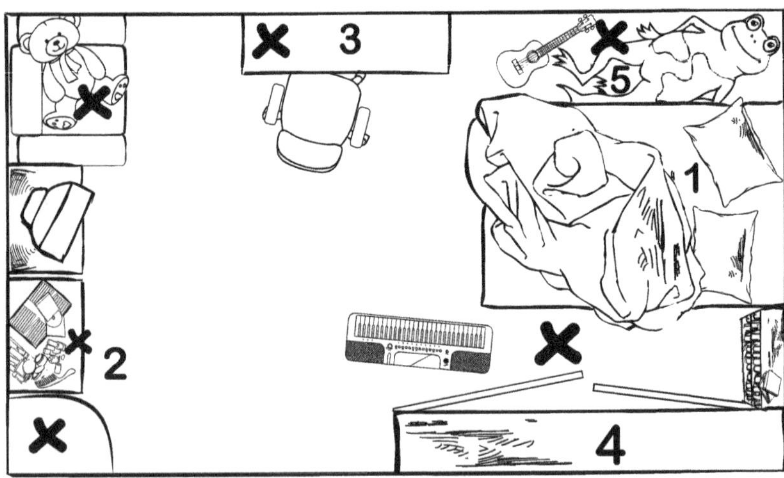

Figure 1

Figure 1 is a diagram of Alex's room and the five zones in the Ba-Gua that are addressed in this chapter.

The following is a description of the content of five zones in the Ba-Gua as they correspond with the area in Alex's bedroom. The analysis that follows provides a more in-depth interpretation. The areas marked with ✖ in the diagram (Figure 1) indicate significant clutter spots.

 # 1 Creativity Zone: Alex's bed was in the creativity section of her room. The mattress pad she was sleeping on had originally belonged to her deceased grandmother. She had been sleeping on it ever since her grandmother passed away. According to Alex, her grandmother was a very "sad and lonely person and possibly mentally ill." There were also posters, pictures, an image of the animated cartoon character SpongeBob SquarePants, and an old quilt that hung over her head.

 # 2 Skills/Wisdom/Inner Knowing Zone: The door to the bedroom entered here. A "No Trespassing" sign was affixed on the front of it. The door itself was not very inviting and had writing all over the front. Walking into the room, I was greeted by a dresser that was crammed with CDs, photographs, and things that, according to Alex, she was not using frequently.

Alex had the dresser since she was a child and told me, "I hate it." It was toppling over with knick-knacks, jewelry, makeup, stuffed toys, and many empty little boxes. Clothing hung from the knobs on the dresser. Empty bags were scattered around, and the beginnings of unfinished projects lined this area. This big clunky piece of furniture box was creating an obstruction to the energy flow and all the clutter was clogging her intuition.

 # 3 Fame/Self-Image: This area was where Alex's desk was positioned. Here, Alex would sit with her back to the door, exposed and not in the command position. Instead, this placement was contributing to her feeling more insecure and disempowered. At one point in the interview, she mentioned that her boyfriend "took a lot of her priv-  ileges away." It would probably be more accurate to say that she was not in command of her life and was giving her power away. Because she did not have a view of the door, she could not see the opportunities that were available to her. Plus, her desk was cluttered.

#4 Helpful People: This area contained many items and was very congested. It contained a bookshelf overflowing with books and awards from much earlier years. Alex's keyboard was crammed in this section, but it was doubtful she was using it in this tight space. Furthermore, in this area was a portion of the closet that contained Alex's mother's scrapbooks  and photo albums, books, and even some of her old clothing.

#5 Relationships/Friendships: A gigantic, oversized frog that Alex had made with her deceased grandmother was dominating this area. Her guitar was also placed here, but the toy frog was overshadowing her music. No space existed here for anything else.

One month later: When I came back to visit Alex, her room makeover was still a work in progress. Figure 2 reflects some of the changes made to her room.

Alex had implemented some of my suggestions but also had taken the initiative to make some of her own changes in the placement of objects in her space. "I've been decluttering stuff one piece at a time." The room contained substantially less clutter than during our first visit. She reported that she had started making friends and was no longer pushing people away from her. She was opening her circle and enjoying life more.

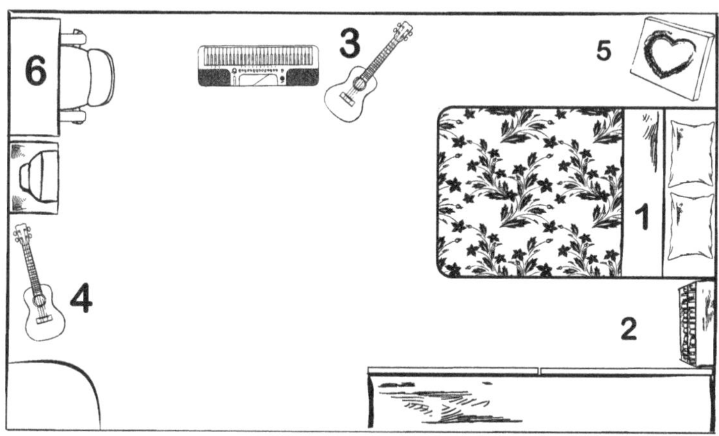

Figure 2

The most significant change was that Alex had removed most of the posters, toys, empty boxes, stuffed animals, and the big bulky furniture. The changes in the five areas noted in the diagram were as follows:

 # 1 Creativity: All posters that were hanging over her head were removed. Ivory-colored sheets temporarily replaced the previous bright pink bedding (she was still searching for the ideal bedding) and reflected a more mature version of Alex. She also threw out the mattress pad belonging to her deceased grandmother, along with its heavy energy. Phew!

 # 2 Helpful People: The bookshelf contained much less clutter and showcased her awards. The entire area was much less congested. However, the closets were still jammed with her mother's books and photo albums.

 # 3 Power/Self-Image/Fame: This wall was painted red. In feng shui, red denotes power and courage, which reflected Alex stepping into her power. She also placed her guitar and keyboard here to symbolize her intention to be recognized for her music and have her own record label.

 # 4 Skills/Wisdom/Inner Knowing: She removed the dresser from childhood that she "hated" and that was accumulating clutter, and cleaned the boxes from the floor that were blocking the flow of good energy and obstructing her inner knowing. She also placed another guitar here.

#5 Relationship/Friendships: Alex removed the gigantic stuffed frog that was hanging all by itself from the wall and dominating this section, and replaced it with an image of a heart, symbolically making room for new heart-centered friendships.

#6 Prosperity Zone: Alex moved her desk to the Prosperity Zone, which was a more favorable position than having it in the Fame Zone with its back to the door.

Five months later: Alex shared that she was still clearing clutter and had gotten sidetracked. Her mother had finally cleared out all her things from Alex's closet. According to Alex, quite a few changes had occurred in her life. Alex said, "I went from only having one or two close friends to hanging out with different people every day or so. My confidence has really gotten a boost, so now I have about seven or eight people who want to go out with me. It's really bizarre!"

Six months later: A month later, when I checked in with Alex again and asked her if I could come to take the final photos of her room, she told me that she was no longer living at her parent's home. When her parents' divorce was finalized, she had moved in with her father. Alex needed more autonomy. She said, "Mom gets overinvolved, and I want more independence."

Ten months later: In another phone conversation with Alex, she reported that she was happily living with her father. She said that she was still holding on to some belongings in boxes and planned on "throwing things away." She told me, "The boxes have sat in storage for three months, and I realized that I wasn't accessing anything out of them. I only remembered a few of the things that were in the boxes." In addition, she said that her room currently had only a few items in it and was not very cluttered.

She told me that she had created a real community and made friends. She said, "I don't feel like I push people away anymore." The separation from her mother had given Alex emotional space to significantly nourish their relationship. "Now, we're close," she said.

I asked Alex, "What's different about being with your dad?"

"Dad really keeps me grounded. My cat is happy too. Dad doesn't have a lot. We are okay with what we have. He can't really afford to get more stuff."

When I asked her why she did not end up moving into the dorms at college, she said it was cheaper for her to live with her dad and she was helping him out with the rent.

Alex informed me that she had recently met a new guy who was a musician and that she felt very inspired by him. She said,

> He is the most self-disciplined person I've ever met. I'm inspired to do better and do everything I want in my life. I went on a date with him and we had a blast. This guy is so spiritual and treats women well.

She told me that she was connecting with her spirituality and had begun reading spiritual discourses; this was quite a contrast from when we first met. Both of her parents followed a spiritual path in which she had been steeped from an early age. She had resisted following her parents' path and had wanted to do her "own thing." Now, she was ready to embrace the spirituality with which she was raised and redefine it for herself. She had turned a new leaf in her life, spiritually.

Fun Shway Assessment

When I began my work with Alex, her room was in a state of disarray. The Chi was stuck and congested. Alex shared that since she had moved back to the house after her stay with her boyfriend, she had "reverted back to a sad place inside." I was not surprised. Many things covered the floor and were scattered throughout the room, which may have been depressing her energy.

I felt like there were layers upon layers of pain, sadness, and grief that hadn't been released. Perhaps the attachment to the items from a "happier time" helped her feel a sense of containment while her family life was literally falling apart. Her parents were divorcing and had declared bankruptcy. Keeping herself frozen in a younger version ensured a temporary sense of safety, while unfortunately arresting her self-development and keeping her feeling trapped.

Alex was aware that holding onto all this stuff was a metaphor for living in the past and an unwillingness to embrace the present moment. She said, "Which is basically what this whole room symbolizes. I don't want to let it go because it reminds me of how I was when I was fourteen and fifteen. I don't like parts of my life now. I think things were a lot simpler back then, and I wish I could go back."

She was having a challenging time moving through the adolescent stage and transitioning into adulthood. Keeping her room stuck in a time warp did not make her happier, but only had the opposite effect. She was not able to access her power and live a fuller life. Her ex-boyfriend was controlling and troubled.

Catering to his needs was another way of avoiding herself. Fun Shway measures were taken to create more energy flow, help Alex move out of stagnation, and lessen her sentimental attachment to possessions. She released a significant amount of clutter and stuck energy. "I've always had the issue that I have lots of sentimental stuff that I want to keep, but it's not serving me. Trying to figure out what to do has been difficult." During our second session, I asked her, "What do you need to do to identify clutter versus items that have value for you?" She responded, "I need to be honest with myself. Having a cleaner room helps me stay more energetic."

She also got rid of the couch and said she bagged lots of her clothing that she was no longer wearing. Although she was not capable of fully releasing all the things that were holding her down, she transferred much of it into the garage; this was still progress and she was creating space between her attachment to her belongings. It is possible that removing the gigantic green stuffed frog from the Relationship/Friendship Zone in her room was one of the things that catalyzed more space in her life for new relationships.

The other thing that struck me as very telling was the mattress pad that had belonged to her grandmother. The function of a mattress is to be supportive. Feng shui holds that objects have a life and a history and can influence a person's experience. According to Alex, her grandmother abandoned her mother and "all of the siblings when they were children." As a result, her mother had to take care of "everyone." The mattress was holding the energy of a grandmother who was sad and lonely and who could not support her own family, and most likely herself. This history was being mirrored in Alex's own life. She was having a hard time supporting herself to manifest her vision for her life. She kept going back to her ex-boyfriend and was having a hard time moving forward. Moreover, this "dead" energy was stifling her creativity and self-expression, which were being exhausted by the hopelessness and depression that were associated with the mattress.

She shared that she had been sleeping on the mattress since her grandma died. Feng shui and space-clearing practitioners follow the principle that all objects in a person's space are imprinted with energy. According to Kingston (1999),

"Everything that happens in a building is recorded in the walls, floors, furniture, and objects in the space. This builds up in layers, in much the same way as grime does, except that we cannot see it, and it affects us in profound ways." (p. 7)

Moreover, we spend a third of our lives in bed and this bed was not energetically supporting Alex. I initiated a Space Clearing to clear the old energy from the mattress. We started with the Bed Smacking process described in chapter 12. I also encouraged Alex either to get another mattress pad or simply to stop using this one. The new ivory bedding that she purchased after this session reflected a more mature aspect of her personality.

One of the biggest changes to the space was that Alex removed from the wall most of the posters and items with which she no longer identified. When I asked her how the process felt for her, her response was, "It was difficult. I have an attachment to pretty much everything on the wall. It's like they were my babies, and I'm losing them. I haven't actually thrown them away."

Alex explained that she moved everything into the garage because she did not have "the guts to throw it out yet." I praised her for the courage it took and acknowledged that she had created space between herself and the stuff. "I've stopped myself from putting anything else up on the wall," she said. Once everything was removed from the walls, she painted the Power/Self-Image/Fame wall red, which is a symbol of power in feng shui and represented her emergence into a more empowered version of herself.

These were huge improvements for Alex, considering her previous level of attachment to her things. I encouraged her to live with bare walls for a while and experience the feeling of living without so much visual stimuli.

Alex's mother also cleared her things out of Alex's closet and had a garage sale for many of her possessions that she had been accumulating for decades. Throughout the process of letting go and freeing herself of her belongings, Alex cleared so much energy in her room that she essentially loosened the enmeshed ties with her mother and freed herself from living with her.

Fun Shway was the catalyst for change and initiated the process of release and realignment. From my own experience, I can say with certainty that when clients trust the process, it usually takes them where they need to go.

Both Amy and Alex began a journey that included letting go of outdated modes of self-expression by releasing the things in their space that no longer represented them. They emerged from this experience as more mature, whole, and integrated.

Infusing the space with the power of their own intentions supported them in feeling more in control over their lives. The intention to change one's environment, and the positive results that follow, builds the self-confidence needed to improve other areas of life.

The room becomes a microcosm, a container for both internal dynamics and their manifested equivalents in life. By tracing spatial configurations of objects and the symbols in the room to their analog representation in life, anyone can design a room that reflects the life they want to lead. This dynamic is evident in the previous makeovers.

When Alex and Amy asserted their will over their spaces, they gained a partnership with the universe and a sense of co-creative empowerment, as opposed to feeling a victim of circumstance. Fun Shway cleared the way for more of their true selves to shine.

The goal of Fun Shway is to bring harmony into your space and into your life. Once you begin to put the principles into practice, you will find your life is improving. I hope that you will use the teachings from this book and make the life that you desire. It might not happen all at once, but once you practice Fun Shway, your energy will naturally shift, and a higher version of your life's destiny will follow.

AFTERWORD

Fun Shway in Challenging Times

Life will always present us with challenges beyond our control, whether that be a pandemic, a natural disaster, or a loss of any kind, large or small. These challenges will force some people to turn inwards and hide from life, while others will demonstrate their resiliency, strength, and sovereignty over the one place they do have control—their inner experience.

During times of uncertainty, one's room can be a respite—a place to find balance, replenish energy, and connect to a higher truth. This space can be a sacred container that cradles our inner experience. We need these sacred containers in order to powerfully move through life's challenges.

When we start to view things symbolically, we approach life as a sacred vessel, where all things contained within, even the most mundane, have a spark of the divine. As we navigate the unfolding events of life, relating to our spaces, not only the physical but also the mental, emotional, and spiritual, will help us find peace and joy in our journeys.

Life is rarely if ever experienced as perfect. But within the seeming imperfections lies harmony. Within the uncertainty lies beauty. Beauty can also be born from chaos; and from chaos comes cosmos. As we deepen in our co-creative powers with the universe and transform our rooms with Fun Shway, the interconnected tapestry of life unfolds. Inside-out becomes outside-in and we become more tolerant, wiser, and compassionate beings. May Fun Shway serve as a flashlight into the uncharted territories of your inner and outer worlds. May every day feel like a gorgeous and grand adventure.

ACKNOWLEDGMENTS

A special token of gratitude goes to all my teachers, here and beyond, but especially to my feng shui professor and dear friend, Elnathan Batoon. Thank you for making feng shui so fascinating, fun, and simple to learn.

Thank you to Daniel, who had the insight to encourage me to study feng shui, even when I said, "Why would I do that? I don't want to move people's couches." Little did I know!

Thank you to my creative "Get Your SH!T done" coach, Nicole Miriam Raz. Without your support, attention to detail, dedication, and constant encouragement, it may have taken another decade to birth this book.

Thanks to Alexis Justice, who has been my guiding light and dear friend since we met in Bali, Indonesia—the magical place where I first received the idea for Fun Shway.

Thanks to Katherine Coder for the many facets of support, encouragement, love, and friendship you've provided me with over the years.

Thank you to Michelle, my younger sister. You've been my biggest cheerleader and the first recipient of Fun Shway.

Thank you to Damona Resnick Hoffman, Dr. Koffler, my feng shui students, clients, and classmates for all your support along the way.

Thank you to my partner who surprises me every day with his keen ability to symbolically look at homes. It's fun to share feng shui with you.

Thank you to my guides and ancestors that are always with me and leading me in the right direction to manifest my destiny.

Finally, to my colorful and loving parents, thank you for insisting that I get a "real job." Without your opposition, I may never have had the chance to rebel against your wishes, stand firm in who I am, and become my own person, as well as a more integrated, funny, and compassionate adult. It took you a decade to warm up to feng shui, let alone pronounce it. I am still not sure if you understand what I do, but at least you have grown to find the humor in it and accept me. I love you.

AUTHOR BIO

Inessa Freya (Inessa Freylekhman, LMFT) is a maestra of feng shui and practitioner of spiritual psychology. She has dedicated her life to helping others heal, awaken, and transform to live in more joyful radiance.

Inessa was intuitive and a truth seeker straight out of the womb. She read her first self-help book, *Codependent No More*, at the age of 12. In high school, she was voted "most likely to write a self-help book." It's no wonder that she was introduced to feng shui after college in the most unlikely of places—Hollywood. Call it universal intervention or destiny, Inessa wound up bringing subconscious design with intention to the corner offices and homes of actors and producers as a casting associate. This led her to leave Hollywood behind to earn two master's degrees, one in Spiritual Psychology from the University of Santa Monica, and her second in Counseling Psychology with an emphasis in Marriage & Family Therapy from Pacifica Graduate Institute. It's this lifelong quest for studying the mind, body, and soul connection—in addition to twenty years of truth seeking—that sets Inessa's unique blend of techniques apart and results in profound shifts and transformations for her clients. She is dedicated to helping others overcome obstacles and live their best lives by integrating the mind, body, and spirit for healing and reconnection to their true selves.

When she's not coaching clients, teaching workshops, or applying her feng shui expertise, Inessa writes and performs humorous stories about her Ukrainian family and feng shui adventures, showcasing her multifaceted talents and genuine love for helping others whilst making them laugh.

Printed in the USA
CPSIA information can be obtained
at www.ICGtesting.com
LVHW092118220624
783785LV00005B/110

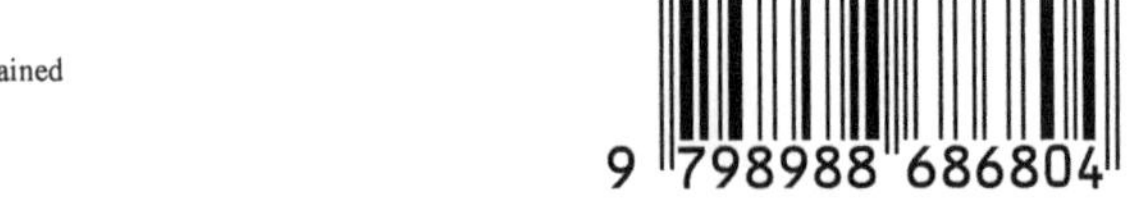

Praise for Fun Shway

"In her fun and informative new book, Inessa Freya tells you how to clear your clutter, feel empowered, and become inspired to create new possibilities! I've experienced her feng shui practice in my own life and I can tell you it had a meaningful effect on my life and on my living space. I give this book five stars!"

—Dr. Wendy A. Suzuki

Professor of Neural Science and Psychology at New York University
Author of *Healthy Brain Happy Life* and *Good Anxiety*

"Inessa Freya has turned the ancient art of feng shui into a real fun experience in the cleverest way. Her book is full of surprises at each corner. From decluttering your space, Inessa leads you to declutter your life and finding a deeper meaning to it. A real treasure awaits the reader in each chapter. Playful and deep, you will learn the art of being at ease with yourself as you are creating your new environment. I wish every young adult would read this book to bring harmony and balance to their lives."

—Micheline Nader

Entrepreneur, motivational speaker, and best-selling author of
The Dolphin's Dance and *Leap Beyond Success*

"Inessa is the real deal. With her support, I've used feng shui to completely transform my life. As a mom, I would also recommend her book *Fun Shway: A Feng Shui Guide for Young Adults—Change Your Room, Change Your Life* to help young adults access their best selves, create and maintain healthy relationships, process anxiety, and feel empowered to steer their own paths in life."

—Damona Hoffman

Host of the *Dates & Mates Podcast* and author of *F The Fairy Tale*

"A Must Read. In her new book, *Fun Shway: A Feng Shui Guide for Young Adults—Change Your Room, Change Your Life*, Inessa Freya draws upon the principles of feng shui and psychology to help empower every young adult to navigate life's uncertainties. She outlines the skills for gaining clarity, consciously creating an inspired room, and improving self-esteem in easy ways to understand and implement."

—Dharma Singh Khalsa, MD

Best-selling author of *Meditation as Medicine*

"If you are a young adult, you need this book! Inessa Freya gives beautiful advice to open up new possibilities and discover the ways to make them come true. She helps guide you to balance your room and yourself, to find your passion, and create an amazing life!"

—Jennifer Grace

Clarity Coach and author of *Directing Your Destiny*

"*Fun Shway* is a delightful book that captures the principles of the ancient art of feng shui peppered with spiritual psychology and delivers a system for supporting young adults to use their room as a tool for personal growth and empowerment."

—Brian Whetten, Ph.D.

Author of *Yes Yes Hell No! The Little Book for Making Big Decisions*

"*Fun Shway* shows you how to use your room to your advantage, get rid of clutter, and invite more Chi, the energy that supports your well-being. This is the plan for healthy relationships and to become empowered in your life. I wish I had this when I was younger! A must-read!"

—Raquel Reyna MA Spiritual Psychology

Author of *Are You a Mutant: The Step-By-Step Human Design Guide to Unleash Your Genius, Discover Your Uniqueness, and Thrive During Times of Transformation*. Mystical Human Design Teacher